PREACHER BREATH

Smyth & Helwys Publishing, Inc.
6316 Peake Road
Macon, Georgia 31210-3960
1-800-747-3016

Library of Congress Cataloging-in-Publication Data

Rothaus, Kyndall Rae.
[Sermons. Selections]
Preacher breath : a collection of sermons and essays / by Kyndall Rae Rothaus.
pages cm
Includes bibliographical references.
ISBN 978-1-57312-734-9 (pbk. : alk. paper)
1. Baptists--Sermons. 2. Sermons, American--Women authors. 3. Preaching. I. Title.
BX6333.R68P74 2015
252'.061--dc23

2014036528

Preacher Breath

sermons & essays by
Kyndall Rae Rothaus

To Kelsey and Kaitlyn,
two strong and remarkable women
whom I am honored to call my sisters

contents

preface

í once knew a woman whose clothes always smelled of wine, with a trace of something stronger on her breath. We got along fine, but other folks in the office found her a little loopy, and eventually she was fired from her job for incompetence. While I do not want to make light of a disease, I do want to lift her up as an inspirational image for the profession of preachers: that we might smell to the world like those who have consumed copious amounts of the holy. Or that we might be like those who have *been* consumed so that the breath of God—were anyone lucky enough to get a whiff—would carry our scent. That we might often seem to the straight-laced and stern-faced a little loopy, and that at least a time or two over the course of our lives we would run the risk of getting fired, because if there is never a point in our vocation where we ruffle some self-righteous feathers, then we are doing this business all wrong.

Like morning breath, may there be a pungency to our work that saturates the environments we enter with an essence that cannot be ignored.

I also speak of breath in another sense. Preaching is more than exegesis, more than writing, more than speech-delivering. Preaching is an inhale and exhale of Spirit. There is a lung muscle to the task of preaching that must be exercised and stretched. Without the Spirit breath, we are left with empty words and gospel-dry mouths.

May our preaching invigorate the valley of dry bones, adding flesh to ancient script. May our preaching swirl with the dust of earth, invoke the ruah[1] *of God, and create new things. May our preaching tap into the resurrecting Power that blows through decay like an invigorating wind, stirring up new life in places of former suffocation.*

This is not a book for example sermons of preaching perfection, nor is this a how-to book on making proclamation. This is a book that aspires to be oxygen to the short of breath and whiskey to the uptight and anxious.

If you are a preacher, I certainly wouldn't wish for you to copy what you find me doing here. It would be a great disservice to the world if we missed your voice because you covered it with imitations of another. My words will have failed if they pressure rather than free you, if they make you feel inadequate rather than bolster your worthiness.

If you think you *might* be a preacher (or are supposed to be a preacher someday), well, you probably are one already, so do not think for a minute that these words are not for you or that you could never do this job. The truth is, none of us can do this job, but some of us must develop the guts to try the impossible. So if you are being called to try and fail at speaking of God (because failure is all there really is when it comes to describing the divine), then do not balk, but fall right into it with abandon because the Mystery will catch you, and those of us who already jumped will be your friends.

If you are not a preacher, I encourage you to read this book anyway. Most people of faith are preachers unaware. Something about your life is preaching to someone, somewhere, even though you may never know it. Basically, everyone has preacher breath sometimes. It is an unavoidable aspect of faith, and it is better to think about how you want to breathe on others than never to recognize the force of your own lungs.

This isn't a "here's how to preach" book. This is a "here is how I try to live a whole life as a preacher" story. More than that, it is a "here is how I try to live a whole life. Period." It just so happens that I am a preacher, but if you are in any way seeking to live a whole life too, then maybe we can sojourn together.

May my heartfelt words and my fumbling practices be grace to you.

In the course of creating this book, I originally wrote my ideas about preaching, then came back later and added stories about myself. While writing my stories I consistently fretted, *Is this too personal? What is the point of all this self-talk?* Because if you and I were sitting at dinner, I'd say little about me and ask you lots of questions about you. Yet in these pages I talk profusely about me, which feels oddly one-sided. I finally landed on this conclusion: I am telling the one story I've got—my own. I hope that by reading my story, you will be able to see that while I have some pretty strong thoughts about preaching, about living, and about living-in-God, these thoughts arise from my story and my experiences, and your story may bend you in a different direction.

My tale isn't meant to be prescriptive. It's meant to be real and lived and hopeful to those who read it. The best I can hope for is that even where we differ, my story will intersect with yours in a way that illumines and challenges us both. I am not a preacher who has it all figured out. But I am a preacher. One with passion and conviction and lessons she seems to be learning. Why don't we help one another along this crazy journey toward the well-lived life by exchanging vulnerabilities? I'll go first. (Write me a letter when you're finished reading.)

Grace and peace and inspiration be yours.

Love,
Kyndall Rae Rothaus

1

heart:
purpose in preaching

fOR mY fIRST eXPeRIeNCe at weekly preaching, I did pulpit supply for a twelve-person congregation in the small town of West, Texas, while still in seminary. In addition to preaching on Sundays and keeping up with classes, I held another part-time job as a chaplain in a college dorm. It was a busy time.

Before the interim position, when I was preaching only a handful of times per year, I had the leisure or the torture of abundant time between sermons. I could write and rewrite, edit and reedit, read and reread, and fret about every possible imperfection. During my interim work, I ran out of time for this sort of obsession. The weekly rhythm of preaching forced me out of my addiction to persistent fretting. Often I was left with no other choice but to trust my first instinct, to show up on Sunday, and to preach an only-somewhat-edited draft (yikes!). It was a perfectionist's nightmare: running out of time to control the details.

While I am relieved that my lifestyle today is no longer so hectic, I am grateful for the way that season brought me down to the essence of the work. I did not have time to evaluate to death every little sentence of every single sermon. I only had time to ask myself the questions: Is this sermon bringing Scripture to life? Am I possibly carving out space for people to hear God? If I could give a hopeful "yes" to both questions, then it was a sermon I was going to preach, typos and all.

A few years later, as a full-time pastor for the first time, I went through a second purging of my anxieties. I had only just begun my second year at this church when I endured terrible anguish in my personal life, and once again, my preaching was stripped to its heart and essence. In this case, I was not suffering for lack of time but for lack of reliable inspiration and energy because I was so utterly overcome by grief. *All I could do* was show up to the writing desk, show up to the pencil and paper, show up to the opened Book, show up to the Sunday morning hour. Each and every time I showed up, I felt certain that I had nothing to say and nothing to offer. And yet, somehow, a way was opened. Often at the last minute an idea would strike after hours upon hours of seemingly fruitless wrestling. I had to trust whatever seed came to me in that late hour, because there wasn't time to find another one. Difficult as that season of desolation was, it was yet another purging, bringing me back to the core of preaching, eliminating the egotistical excess that thwarts true work.

The purging process, though painful, is also transformative and essential. We do not learn the heart of our preaching easily or without enduring some hardship, but the challenges we face will serve as a purging. If we allow our struggles to refine us, the difficulties we endure will move us closer to the heart of what we do and why we do it.

This happens differently for different people. I believe every preacher must discover for herself what the heart of preaching is; what is beating at the core of you looks different from what is beating at the core of me. Each preacher has her own specific desire, intent, and purpose to what she is doing. Her passions are bound to overlap with the passions of other preachers, no doubt, but there is a unique twist to each preacher's pulse.

If you are not yet clear on where the "heart" lies for you, I believe that you will gain clarity over time. Follow your own process, and your purpose for preaching will find you. As you begin to recognize what you are most meant to do in a pulpit, the clarity will free you. Knowing what you are meant to reach for (even if it seems you fail to attain it) is a gift to your study, writing, preparation, and delivery. May you ask to be given this gift, to be shown what it is you are meant for. I think if you ask, it will be given to you. Whatever the heart of *your* preaching is, trust it. Live into it. God gave you this heart for a divine purpose.

Over time it has grown ever clearer to me that I am attempting to accomplish exactly two things in preaching. This is my heart when it comes to the pulpit:

1. *To bring Scripture to life.* To me, this means picking up the ancient words that so often seem dead, taking them down from the coffin-shelf, shaking off the dust, and giving them flesh. When I preach, I am putting legs on a text, then giving it a wobbly shove right into the hearts (I hope) of the people.

I do not get to know or control *where* it walks once it leaves me. I am not trying to manipulate a certain experience, insight, or behavioral shift. I do not get to dictate exactly what people hear, where the message will hit their lives, or how they will respond. I do my best to trust that this may happen differently for each individual in the room. In my case, I do not try to guess what people are going through or what they need to hear, because that seems like an undertaking with a small percentage of success. I try instead to believe it down in my bones that the stories of Scripture *can* speak, *do* speak, and *will* speak, and my job is to give them voice in this generation via my own body.

In this regard, I may be different from the average preacher in that I do not *try* to make my preaching connect with my audience. I do not *look* for ways the Scripture might relate to our personal lives or to what is going on in the current cultural climate. I just believe that the Scripture is a living thing, inviting me to dance, and the event of preaching is that moment in the process where the curtain gets drawn back and others get a peek of this odd little jig between an ancient text and one small girl with two left feet.

Often, to my own shock and surprise, this *moves* people. They get caught up in the aliveness of the text too, and before they know it, they are tapping their feet.

As I bring a text to life (or it brings me to life—I never know which), there are times when I momentarily collapse into self-doubt that says I am doing this work all wrong. I am not systematic, nor could I tell you what the "application" of any one sermon is. I hate the question, "What is your sermon *about?*" because I never know how to answer. I would hardly make a passing grade if I were turning in exegetical prep work for preaching class. That is not to say that I do not study the text, that I have forfeited what I learned in seminary, or that I preach in a scattered, disorganized way. But I do not necessarily follow rules well. I like to think outside the box, I use as much, if not more, imagination than I do scholarship, and I just don't *feel* very preacher-ish.

Most weeks, I decide *I must be doing it wrong. These words are stupid. I am going to embarrass myself in front of everyone. Why am I in this profession?*

But then I remind myself of what I am trying to do: to bring the text to life. Not explain everything about it. Not teach a biblical history lesson (or a church history lesson for that matter.) Not give a motivational speech. Not change people's behavior. Not change the world. Not save a soul. If any of those other things happen, that is a bonus, but those things happen by God's Spirit, not by my effort.

2. To open a roomier space for folks to encounter God. In my preaching, I hope to wriggle people loose from the constricted places that keep them from God. Preaching is like making a clearing, like removing obstacles for people with overgrown paths, and for this reason preaching will always be relevant. After all, who has ever had an unobstructed path to God at all times? This is the business of helping to eliminate what distracts and shine a light on what we are being invited into. With preaching, I want to open closed eyes and remove plugs from stopped ears. I choose to believe that when people show up for worship, this is what they really crave deep down, whether they know it or not: to encounter God for real, even if the encounter is small and subtle and fleeting.

Preaching is like repositioning God into the people's line of vision, or at least sneaking God into their periphery. We all come to the hour of worship with a variety of mixed motives, both good and bad, but I think the hunger for God is always there, even when we are masking it, pushing it aside, feeling afraid of the hunger pains, or expending our energy acquiring other things. At all times, deep within, we are hungry for God.

Preachers do not, of course, satisfy or fill people up with each sermon. It would be presumptuous, dangerous, and silly to think of preaching in that way. We are not supplying the food. But we are often whetting the appetite, helping people shed unhealthy desires, normalizing the reality that God does not often show up in the ways we thought our hunger demanded, giving people a taste of what *can* happen in God, and propelling them toward a daily, godly gluttony of feeding their souls. *We* do not feed the souls. This is not a circus and people are not our pets. They are human beings with roaring, raging, and rambunctious faith journeys of their own. They do not need us to feed them, nor could we if we tried. They come to worship for some direction, hoping for a bit of sacred encounter, as ready as they can be to receive a measure of grace and a sense of the holy.

Having these two humble aims in mind when I work with a text is immensely helpful. It is a little like putting your hand over your heart in a crisis and reminding yourself that you're still alive. I want to panic some weeks, staring blankly at a Scripture and feeling paralyzed by the potential to screw up this thing called preaching. Then I whisper gently to my panic, "Bring the Scripture to life. Try to help people see God. Bring the Scripture to life. Try to help people see God. All you can do is try it. Try it and pray. Those are your jobs, Kyndall. Not to save the world. Just to do these small things on behalf of the world."

This is what I think we should remember as preachers: Do not try to do too much. Do *not* do too little. Be a good and faithful steward as the groundskeeper of sacred space and the timekeeper of the holy hour, but beyond that, let the Spirit do what she will and *relax.*

Who Taught You How to Climb a Tree?

Luke 19:1-10 (All Saints' Day,
Covenant Baptist Church)

"He wanted to see who Jesus was but on account of the crowd, he could not" (Luke 19:3).

I don't know if any other line could more accurately describe the entire human religious condition than that one: "They wanted to see who God was but on account of the crowd, they could not. *We* wanted to see who Jesus was but on account of the crowd, we could not."

Whether you are short or tall, have perfect vision or need glasses, you know what it is like trying to find Jesus in a crowd, and it ain't easy. There are so many people to cloud our view. There is always one crowd or another waving posters in our faces that declare Jesus supports their cause, or their politics, or their war. In this country, there is a red Jesus *and* a blue Jesus. There is even a purple Jesus for the moderates. There is a green Jesus for the eco-friendly, a white Jesus, for, well, white people. For every cause under the sun, every stance and every platform, there is a Jesus who fits the bill.

And there's nothing unreasonable about wanting and hoping that Jesus looks and thinks like we do; if he did, then he'd be sure to love us. We'd get to be his favorites. But move three levels or so beneath your insecurities, and it turns out that you want to know who Jesus is for real, unadorned by what you need him to be to feel okay about yourself. *You want to know Jesus as he really is.* You want to know the real thing, and then you want to find out that no matter how different he is from you, he loves you like a favorite anyway, and that no matter how wide the gap between his righteousness and yours, you've got something of his image irrevocably within you, and there is hope, always hope, for you.

Now Zacchaeus, being short-legged and all, was having trouble seeing through the crowds to the real Jesus. He could have plopped down on a rock and fantasized what Jesus looked like—Jesus probably looked like him, in his head. And he may have done just that for a spell, and that is why he was late and ended up stuck at the back of the crowd. He had stayed home too long, where he was comfortable, *imagining* Jesus walking through his city, imagining who Jesus was, how he sounded, what he would say. Maybe Zacchaeus nearly daydreamed the day away. But, comfortable or not, this wasn't ultimately very satisfying, to make God in one's own image. Didn't require much adventure out of him, didn't take any imagination, brought very little lasting joy.

So at some point, Zacchaeus got up from the couch and realized he wanted to see who Jesus was. He decided to find out, but (as we know) on account of the crowd, he could not. To me, this is where the story gets downright delightful.

Zacchaeus did not just stand there at the back of the throng, waiting for the rumors of Jesus to pass down the line and finally reach his ears like a religious game of telephone. He did not ask some friend at the front of the crowd to snap a photo and text it to him. He did not read a book on what it is like to sit at the feet of Jesus. He did not attend a "Who Is Jesus, Really?" seminar. He did not take a class or phone a friend or watch a documentary on Netflix.

The man climbed a tree.

This grown man, this businessman, this rich man, this I-used-to-care-what-everyone-thought man, this I-have-status man, this I-want-to-see-Jesus man hiked up his long garments and wrapped his possibly aging limbs around the bark of branches and *climbed* like a monkey or like a child but nothing like a respectable, well-put-together man.

What's not to love about a story like this one, about the spirituality of tree climbing? If Jesus hadn't come to Zacchaeus, he would have crowd-surfed to Jesus. He had become like one uninhibited in his seeking. Of course, the crowd wasn't too pleased.

They were a little scandalized by the whole affair, especially by Jesus' positive response to it, and this is the part of the story where we are reminded that Zacchaeus is a man with a past. But that's of little consequence! Climbing the tree propelled Zacchaeus right into the abundance of his future, and by the time Jesus had looked him in the eye and he had shimmied down in haste, he was more than ready to repent. Have you ever heard of a more eager, happy repenter?

The Gospel of Luke is always trying to help us get the picture: that repentance isn't penance; it's a party—a happy, joyous occasion for the one who was lost, then found, and for the one who does the finding. It's all over the place in Luke: the lost coin, the lost sheep, the lost son. Now it is the lost tax collector whom Jesus finds in a tree of all places. While everyone else is offended by this discovery and the subsequent embrace, it does not stop Jesus or Zacchaeus from smiling or from enacting the man's salvation.

Today is All Saints' Day, and when we hear the word "saint," we tend to think of saintly people, the kind with figurative halos, few mistakes, admirable consistency, and Christ-like demeanor throughout their lives. But as we remember and commemorate and give thanks today for the saints, I ask you not just to think of all the nearly perfect people you have known, but also not to forget who taught you how to climb a tree. Do not forget the person who taught you to live passionately, to break decorum to seek the holy.

Who was it, with their quirky eccentricities, that taught you not to follow the crowd but to march to the beat of a different drum? Who in your life wasn't afraid to live large, but when they erred and knew that they erred, they repented fourfold and with joy? Making amends is a lost art in this world, so if you have known someone with the courage to enact reconciliation—even if it was near the end of his or her life after 5,000 mistakes—that is a person to learn from and emulate.

Often we are most affected not by the seemingly put-together people in our lives but by the broken people who nevertheless choose courage and risk, who keep seeking, keep learning, keep growing, keep getting more generous, keep apologizing when apologies are called for but never apologize for living boldly. It is the Zacchaeus-like saints who teach us that though God may be different from our understanding, we have nothing to fear in reaching toward God, that in our reaching, we will find that we are loved, that we are saved, that we are given the energy to change.

And this is the blessed irony of it all: though the swarming crowds keep us from seeing and knowing God, it is almost guaranteed that we will not find God without the help of the individuals who point us to God. If it weren't for Zacchaeus in a tree, giving us permission to do the unexpected, if it weren't for the unlikely saints setting us free to be ourselves in search of God, if it weren't for *people* bearing something of God's image right before our eyes, we might never know the love of God any other way.

In gratitude for all of them, Amen.

Finding the Christ in Christmas

Luke 1:46-55 (Fourth Sunday of Advent,
Covenant Baptist Church)

"Mary, did you know that your baby boy would one day walk on water?" asks the Christmas song.

It is hard to say what Mary knew, though if the Magnificat tells us anything, before our Lord was any bigger than an acorn inside her womb, *Mary knew things*. There are some things I wish *I* knew.

Was Mary always a poet?

Was she startled by the song as it burst into the open, or had the song been stirring within, unsung, all her life?

Was the melody as haunting, beautiful, and unsettling as the words?

Did heaven stand still and bend its ear to listen?

Scholars often presume that these words we find in Scripture were assigned to Mary after the fact, added by the author for effect, as it hardly seems likely that a poor, uneducated, teenage girl could suddenly erupt in lyrics and melody, as if on Broadway. Unlikely? Yes. It was also unlikely for a woman to conceive by the Holy Spirit. Call me superstitious, but I'm inclined to believe that, if she wanted to, Mary could sing spontaneously and prophetically at the prompt of her cousin's exuberant greeting and a baby's intrauterine leaping. She seemed to have a knack for generating the improbable.

Unlikely indeed that this girl from Nazareth would be the mother of our Lord. Unlikely but fitting that she would be prophet/preacher/poet/proclaimer of the good news of the in-breaking of God into the world. She was, after all, already the vessel. How appropriate that she also served as the mouthpiece. Spokeswoman was a role she shared with her cousin Elizabeth (see v. 43), who passed the prophetic gift to her son, John (poor dad was mute), and it was these three—a post-menopause pregnant woman, an unwed soon-to-be mother, and a leaping fetus—who together formed a trio of proclaimers, putting Christmas into words and movement for the very first time in history.

Was anyone even there to hear them? Or were they alone, singing and leaping in the privacy of Elizabeth's home? It doesn't matter if anyone heard. No one would have believed those out-spoken, hormonal women, patting their bellies and laughing through tears. They were saying the truest thing the world would ever need to hear . . . but who would have believed *them*?

Even if there had been a more believable speaker, with stronger credentials, who would want to listen to such news as this? It was a complete upsetting of the natural order, this talk of scattering the proud, bringing down rulers, lifting up the humble, and send-ing the rich away empty.

It is challenging for us, some two thousand years removed and so nestled in the comfort of privilege ourselves, to appreciate the shock of what this baby meant, to hear the passion of Mary's song, to experience anew the toppling of the settled order. *But every year, Advent and Christmas reintroduce us to the absurdity of the gospel.* God is coming to turn the world upside down, but God is coming not in power and might but in human flesh, as a tiny, helpless baby of humble origin.

To recapture this upheaval, in medieval times people observed the Feast of Fools—a comic festival where popes and bishops were "elected" for the day from among the common people and officials were expected to act like servants. Everything was flipped, and with laughter and parody and gaiety, the people dressed in costume and reenacted the glorious and troubling reversal of Mary's Magnificat. As you can probably imagine, sometimes the church embraced the Feast of Fools into the liturgy, and sometimes the church tried to ban the Feast of Fools as having pagan origins. Inside the church, the oddity of the incarnation magnified by a topsy-turvy carnival was perhaps spot-on, and yet it could get to be too much for the tight-laced clergy.

Can you imagine what such a celebration might look like in our world today? What sort of hilarity might startle us back into awe of the incarnation?

If you're like me, you may have received an e-mail forward or two or perhaps a whole slew of them warning you about the demise of Christmas. It's become so un-Christian, this holiday, and Christians have started warning one another, "Watch out. Don't be fooled. Stand firm. Keep Christ in Christmas." Now, while I don't particularly appreciate the extra e-mails in my inbox, I recognize that we *don't* get a good sense of *who* Jesus is when we walk into the shopping mall this time of year. Despite the holiday décor, the music, the lights, the beaming faces, and the generous, generous sales, I get this eerie sense that all of it is aimed at my pocketbook rather than my heart. It doesn't feel worshipful to me inside the mall, unless, of course, the god is money.

So it seems sensible for Christians to ask and to want to know, "How do we put Jesus back at the heart of the season?" This thing started with him, and now he's barely an afterthought, if he's thought of at all. Surely, as Christians, we need to do something.

There are two basic approaches, in my view, to keeping Christmas sacred. One approach is to take all the cultural Christmasy things—the shopping and the baking and the eating and the snowman-making and the light-seeing and the movie-watching—and insert the name of Jesus in and over them. Open presents in Jesus' name. Make gingerbread in Jesus' name. Shop 'til we drop in Jesus' name. Take family photos in Jesus' name. Send Christmas cards in Jesus' name. Decorate the tree in Jesus' name.

Another approach would be to let all the cultural Christmasy things be. Without angst, let them be what they are: a break from work, a way of being with friends and family, a time for fun and feasting, etc. Play the fool, as it were, as if there were little you could do to bring Christ in. The catch, of course, is that the fool also believes there is little you can do to shut Christ out. As you may remember, there was no room for him in the inn, but he came anyway. You may remember that conception normally takes two, but he came anyway. You may remember that Herod tried to eliminate baby boys entirely, but he came anyway. You may remember that they killed him, but he came back anyway. You couldn't get rid of Christ if you wanted to.

If you allow Christmas to make a fool out of you, it will be because you believe this: *Jesus will be among us*—God with us, Immanuel—this Christmas. That story never changes, never dies, never quits repeating itself, no matter if it's the whole world singing his praises or just two pregnant women swapping stories over swollen bellies. Only a fool is willing to accept the mind-boggling, world-changing smallness of a God-baby.

If you want to find the sacredness of Christmas, perhaps you should leave the crowds, the stores, and the places of power and go looking in stables and forsaken places instead. If not literally, then go there spiritually, on the lookout for the holy. Go to that unlikely place inside yourself where bitterness reigns, and look for something new to be born into it. Sit under the blanket of darkness *long enough* to find that one small rip in the shroud where light is just beginning to poke through. This makes Advent an adventure, like wise men who suddenly embrace the wisdom of fools to follow a star and worship a baby. You are looking for the unexpected, for the quiet arrival of God, for subtle signs of incarnation. You'll accomplish very little by way of reclaiming the culture for Christ, but Christ will reclaim your humble adoration. With rejoicing and laughter, you will find yourself stunned. Rather than speak your mind this Christmas, listen for angelic tidings that will tear your settled view of the world apart. A true Christian Christmas will leave you undone. Its absurdity will rattle you to your bones. The mystery of the incarnation will take you by surprise.

By all means, receive Christ like a baby into your arms. Seek Christ like a shepherd. Listen to the unbelievable promise of angels, who speak of peace and goodwill for all. But don't expect anyone to believe your story. If God wanted to make this stuff more believable, more palatable for the public, more popular to those with power, God could have chosen a different way.

As it were, God chose the insanely impractical way of entering the world as a child, as an outsider, making his first appearance in a stable. There is no forcing God into the spotlight, and there is certainly no preserving God's place of honor, as the cross so aptly taught us. You can only wait for God to come, turning your eyes in the direction you least expect so as not to miss it when he does. You can be a part of that foolish remnant who patiently believes. Advent is about waiting in darkness and retraining your eyes to see anew, and if you do, you will be reintroduced to the absurdity of the gospel yet again. May this week bring you a very merry, very startling Christmas indeed. Amen.

2

SOUL:
fire in preaching

In my experience, eighty percent of the fuel for preaching comes from sources outside the study. I do not mean scouring the countryside or the urbanside for sermon illustrations or the discipline of keeping up with the daily news, though both of these may contribute to the content of a sermon. Personally, I do not expend much energy on either—hunting down illustrations or devouring news reports. Both make me tired and grouchy.

What I mean by fuel is the Energy, the Force, the Inspiration of preaching that comes predominantly *not* from study time or from out-in-the-world time but from desert time, soul time, solitude time, spirit-drenching time, or whatever other name you wish to give it. While a current event might energize you momentarily, a heart-warming story might invigorate you, or a fresh insight into the text might seem to propel you, *none* of these are fuel; they are only substance.

Fuel, which is Spirit, God, Fire, Passion, does not often come lodged in the pages of a commentary or wedged between your magazine and morning cup of coffee. If you are relying on insights, events, or stories to fuel you, you are barking up the wrong tree. The right tree is the shade of Divine Presence, and there is little you *do* with shade other than notice it, sit with it, receive it, and appreciate it.

The primary task of preaching is to feed your soul, because every other source will eventually run dry. With enough skill, you can mold and manipulate the material you find in the world and in a text to form a worthy sermon, but you cannot keep up this sham for long. The thing that is meant to carry the sermon out into the hearts of people is nothing short of Divine Power. You are meant to tap into this deeper current that flows beneath the surface. You are meant to spend your time digging, digging, digging the well and then gulping, gulping, gulping its waters. Little else will matter if you do not first drink.

How to feed your soul is not necessarily obvious in that it is not always the overtly religious things that do the trick. How to feed your soul *is obvious*, however, in that *if you pay attention to your life, you will begin to know intuitively what feeds you.* Reading a theological treatise or the latest book on how to form small groups in your church may not be the fodder you deeply need. It may help, but is it what you need the most? Perhaps what you need the most is to read some poetry, a good novel, or a collection of short stories. What you need is to paint, to hike, or to sing. You might need to listen to music, admire a sunset, or hold an infant close enough to smell her baby-fresh skin. Maybe you need to go rock-climbing or kayaking or dancing or bird-watching or seashell collecting. Maybe you need to climb a tree or draw with a box of colored pencils or have yourself a good long laugh. You need to do the things that reawaken your sense of wonder, deepen your gratitude, rekindle your imagination, and invite your inner child out to play.

Of course, some preachers are too flippant about the sermon-writing process, and that is neither useful nor responsible. But those of us with a strong work ethic can sometimes overemphasize our study, effort, and editing as the most important thing, then fling up a last-call panic prayer, "And God be with me." We hope for God to rush in and fill the holes where we are lacking, to make up for what we missed. The Spirit is an afterthought, added on after all our striving. Instead, we must reclaim a way of being that starts with Spirit. What a relief if we can stop wasting so much time on what does not ultimately feed us and start reclaiming what is essential after all.

Preaching is work. There is no way around that if you want to be a good steward of the word you are called to speak. But preaching is also play. Preaching is expression of soul, and *if there is no soul* to express, you had better stop everything and feed your soul, or your preaching is doomed from the start.

This is all the more crucial when your world is rocked by tragedy in some way, and all of us get rocked on occasion. When I was in the throes of grief, my friend had me use her essential oils.

"I know what you're thinking," she said as she anointed my wrists with the fragrance. "*My marriage is falling apart and you want me to smell oils?* Yes. Yes, that's exactly what I want you to do," she stated emphatically.

Oh. So this is self-care.

This was a revelation to me, that self-care can be oh-so-tiny. Sometimes from where you sit the sky is falling, and the only thing you know how to do with the next five minutes is eat some chocolate. Pretend you are recovering from Dementors (yes, that's a Harry Potter reference), or just eat it without knowing how it will possibly help. But if it feels remotely helpful, eat the damn chocolate and don't you dare count calories.

Self-care also means letting yourself have the struggle and feel the pain. We must stop thinking we are meant to power through adversity. We are meant to be *human*: to struggle, to feel, to wail, to question, to thrash, and yes, eventually to thrive, but it is fake thriving if you skip all the other steps. The other steps can be horrific, which is why we understandably avoid them, but there are a thousand small things that will see us through if we choose to enter the rugged terrain of our real souls.

Once you're ready to engage this deep soul work, it can be bewildering to know where to begin. We've been stuffing away the shadow parts of ourselves for so long that it sometimes feels impossible to begin—diving in and facing our "muck." Don't force it. There is no rush. Just be *open* to self-honesty, and the path will present itself. Life events will inevitably bring muck to the surface. If you missed the last opportunity to face your suffering head-on, you undoubtedly will be given another chance. Then, when it comes, take it one step at time. Be exceedingly patient with yourself, but do step forward. Your soul will thank you later.

When I don't have a clue what to do next (which happens to me regularly, not just when tragedy strikes), instead of forcing myself into a premature answer, I try to tend to my soul. Here are some of the things I do instead of forcing answers: make hot tea, listen to a violin, burn incense, light candles, talk to a friend, walk in the woods, make a gratitude list, ask for help, write poetry, go somewhere new, go somewhere familiar, journal, eat comfort food, drink wine. It is absolutely necessary to stop trying to fix things for a while, or it is likely that the solution I conjure up from my anxiety will be a plan that shrinks my soul somehow. And often, once I stop focusing directly on the confusion, clarity catches me by surprise.

You might not know what works for you when you are stuck. You might not know *yet*. But find what gets you in touch with yourself and helps your soul breathe more expansively. The answers you are looking for will come. The guidance will come. The peace will come. What you need most rarely arrives when you are frantically scurrying, desperately faking it, or anxiously grasping at what you don't yet have. Slow down. As Christina Baldwin says, "Move at the pace of guidance." Be attentive to your soul. Not negligent. Not put out. Just gentle and attentive.

I know some of you are thinking, "I don't have *time* to go at a slower pace." Yes, I know. Work, kids, life—it is too much. Maybe before you can say yes to your soul, you will have to practice saying no to other things. Whoever you are, wherever you are, the right pace will eventually be accessible to you if you stay open to it, but of course it will always be hit and miss for most of our lives—sometimes on track, sometimes off. The goal isn't perfection but awareness and gentle correction. The goal is to be awake and to keep waking up. The goal is to never sleepwalk through life again. The goal is to open your eyes.

A friend recently told me that meditation can be a single deep breath. The goal is to keep breathing deeply, to periodically inhale with purpose so that the oxygen reaches you. Keep stretching out and touching your soul; brush up against it periodically, daily, every time you can.

The Blaze

2 Corinthians 4:1, 6-11 (George W. Truett
Theological Seminary, Baylor University)

It is a terrific honor to be with you today, and it is a terrifying privilege to attempt a meaningful word on behalf of the worshiping people, this one small moment in our rather grandiose scheme to consort with God. We preachers never do it justice, and yet I am grateful for this opportunity to fail once more at speaking of God, and I pray that it might be a beautiful shortcoming we behold here together today.

I came here to tell you that there are things they do not teach you in seminary. Such as how to be minister. You can learn tools and theology and theories, but to be a minister in the thick of things, well, you cannot learn that inside these walls, and this is what we have to reckon with—walking out these doors into a world we do not know how to face.

I don't mean to be an alarmist; it is a wonderful world full of adventure. All I'm saying is this is where you pack your bags for the journey, but each and every trailblazer by necessity learns on the fly and becomes who they are as they are hacking through the brush—not before.

I'm not belittling the bag-packing. You will not survive without a water bottle, good solid sustenance for the road, a stash of survival tips, and the like. Do not underestimate the value of what you receive here in seminary.

I'm only saying you're not a trailblazer until you blaze a trail.

I've been a real-life pastor for a whopping two years, so I've hardly the expertise to tell you much, but I can tell you what's happened to me since leaving this wonderful place. It's been a delightful surprise and scary as hell.

I came out from here pretty equipped: I had brilliant and kind professors and worthy classmates, and I worked hard to absorb and integrate all I could. I took seminary seriously, and seminary took me into its folds and shaped my mind and my practice into something useable for the kingdom.

Then I graduated, and I arrived next at the most beautiful, peaceful, wonderful little church I could imagine, as if I were living a fairy-tale version of ministry. It's a quaint building set among five wooded acres of serenity. The place has a magical feel to it, as if fairies lived on our grounds, and of course I mean this in a Christian sense.

I knew how to preach and kinda-sorta how to pastor when I got there, but I didn't know how to be me and I didn't know how to live with myself, so full of doubt and tension and anxiety and worry. I didn't know how to bring my messy self into the church and how to minister authentically out of the center of me. I did not quite know how to feed my soul.

Because in seminary you learn crucial information—how to exegete a passage, how to offer pastoral care, maybe how to run a meeting—but it takes a while beyond all that to learn how to read your own soul, how to be a pastor to yourself, how to manage the mayhem inside of you. And this inner work is the absolute most important thing you will do as a minister, ever. You've got to have the biblical knowledge, the theological knowledge, the ministerial sensitivity, the work ethic, etcetera—those things are like the parameters that steer and guide and keep us from veering too far off track. We need them.

But no amount of information, insight, or skill will provide you the spark and the sustenance to be a conduit of the Holy Spirit. I think that, in the daily grind of ministry, we almost forget that we are handling fire by mingling with God and by brushing shoulders with God's people. That there is this extraordinary power inside our bodies. Call it Spirit or Resurrection or the Light that Shines in Darkness or the Face of Jesus Christ, but it has been entrusted to us, and it is by God's mercy that the Fire hasn't burned us all up into a pile of ash.

There is no studying you can do that will teach you how to handle fire or how to channel it. Not even a book on prayer or a working knowledge of spiritual practices. The only things we can really do as fire-handlers are (1) keep a lookout for burning bushes as we walk through life, (2) add fuel to the flames wherever we spot a fire inside ourselves, (3) be reverent before a blaze, and (4) never, ever, ever substitute anything counterfeit for the real spark.

All your knowledge, all your talent, all your strategies, all your grades, and all your degrees are inflammable. They will not ignite. You have to strike the match beneath your soul to do the work of God, and this is what you will do and learn how to do bit by bit outside these walls. Amid all the tests and essays, our professors have done their best to slip us gasoline underneath the table, but none of that will matter if we do not do the more challenging work of detonating out in the world, again and again.

The other thing that happened to me after I started ministry is that my marriage began crumbling, and let me tell you, I did *not* learn how to deal with that in Life and Work of the Pastor with Dr. Creech. Texts and Traditions wasn't much help either, come to think of it. Eventually my marriage disintegrated completely. This was uncharted territory, unexplored, unknown, unfamiliar, and absolutely terrifying in its darkness. As you well know without me saying it, nothing prepares you for tragedy and grief. Grief always comes unexpectedly, always throws you off balance, always catches you unaware. Even if you suspected its coming, it doesn't matter. It bowls you right over, and if you are human at all, you land on your face for a time when grief comes barreling through your door.

I did not know what to do except to keep my eyes peeled for burning bushes and fledging fires, just any kind of flame at all, really. In other words, my work became to spot Grace wherever I could, however small it appeared, and to honor it. Also, to aggressively feed my soul—at all costs, to do what feeds me, to practice what Anne Lamott calls radical self-care. And to be authentic, even in the midst of pain, to figure out how to be both genuinely and tastefully vulnerable. These are things they cannot teach you in seminary, because you can't learn them, *really* learn them, until you are living them, learning your lessons one agonizing decision at a time.

You think you get into the business of ministry to form others. But really, the business of ministry is to form you. You're not going to lead anyone anywhere unless you're out there yourself, forging a way for your own fragile soul in the midst of a broken world. You're not going to catch any part of the world on fire unless you *keep breathing oxygen* over your own small, God-given flame. It is the most important work you do—the care of your soul, the tending of your flame. It comes before strategizing, before planning, before preaching, before meeting with people, because if we've lost hold of the treasure, we are just empty clay jars with nothing to give, and no wonder we're so tired and stressed and grumpy and have writer's block and lack the imagination to think of anything better to do with our clergy friends than complain about parishioners.

Look. It gets tough, I know. None of us is ever connecting to Spirit all the time. None of us have figured this spirituality thing out. All I am saying is that we've got to always, always, always return to reaching for Spirit and quit for good this self-sufficient nonsense. Too often we get tired and we push ourselves through the exhaustion, bullying our spirit into submission rather than paying attention to the S.O.S. flag our whole body is waving wildly in our face. There is so much I don't know, but this is one thing I am clear about: there is an extraordinary power that belongs to God. It doesn't come from us. So why do we keep expecting miracles to emerge from our scurrying rather than doing whatever it takes to clear ourselves into an empty vessel, open and available for God's filling?

Just like everybody else, there is a lot I am facing in ministry that I don't know what to do about. It's all over the Internet these days how millennials are leaving the church in droves, and theories are cropping up everywhere about how to reverse the trend before half our churches die out. You would think I would have some special insight into this troubling dilemma, seeing as how I am a millennial myself, but all that means is that it is often a tough job to keep myself in the church, much less anybody else. My congregation, which is wonderful and magical and inspiring, is shrinking, and I don't know what to do about it. I don't know. I also don't know how to save marriages or how to keep children from dying or how to stop cancer from hitting families. I don't know.

That's the thing about trailblazing, otherwise known as ministry. There is no map, no instruction sheet. No one is out ahead, telling us what to do with the church in this generation at this frightening time in our personal lives. We're just hacking at brush, not really knowing if we're getting anywhere, constantly getting smacked in the face with stray twigs and branches, getting tangled up in thorny vines, occasionally blessed by the presence of a brilliant wildflower, but more often than not just plum sick of the smell of our own sweat. Afflicted, but not entirely crushed, you might say.

But I recently heard the writer Christina Baldwin relate a dream where she was at the edge of a wide circle, hacking her way through thick overgrowth toward the middle. It was tiresome, lonely work, and she was ready to give in and give up. But then she noticed that it wasn't until she moved closer to the center that she was able to hear the others who were also fighting their way toward the center. The further she blazed her trail, the closer she got to the other trailblazers.

Sometimes in this work of ministry, we feel like a hot mess, and it gets a little unclear what we are even doing, why we are doing it, and whether it will ever work. But this is what we are doing: We are clearing out what stands between us, what is in the way between us and the people to whom we belong, what stands between us and the throbbing center of human existence, where God's incarnational heart is beating. We are reaching for the center. We are also playing with fire. From all outer appearances, we are just cracked clay jars, but all that clearing work makes a clearing inside of us by which we become roomier vessels for Spirit and for power.

Friends, you are going to leave this place, and you are going to witness wonders no one could have predicted because God is that good. You are going to leave this place and face devastations you hoped never to know because the world is that broken. You are going to leave this place and occasionally think yourself stuck in the minutiae of life because life really is strikingly mundane much of the time. You are going to leave this place and more than once feel as though you don't have a clue what you're supposed to do because this thing called ministry isn't a crossword puzzle with one-word answers; it is a jumble of heartache and hope, mystery and suspense, and doubt-tossed trust.

But we do not lose hope. For it is Mercy that brought us here and Mercy that will see us through. So may we trail-blaze with integrity, passion, un-killable hope, a dying ego, and resurrected wonder. May we move through this world handling fire with clay pot hands and a heart full of firewood. May we be Holy Spirit pyros, every last one of us. Amen.

Idlers and Busybodies

2 Thessalonians 3:4-13 (Covenant Baptist Church)

There was once a girl of the busiest sort who was always scurrying about, bustling from this to that, carried most days by the winds of worry and by the adrenaline of to-do lists and self-imposed deadlines and actual deadlines. She moved to the rhythm of the ever-ticking clock in her brain and was often jolted this way, then that way, by the constant sounding of internal alarms, reminding her of this commitment, that goal, this project-in-waiting, that obligation.

She was a good sort of girl, very reliable, often called efficient, many times named by her colleagues Most Likely to Succeed, though what her success would entail no one could articulate. She was much too busy being mildly successful at everything to be wildly successful at any one dream. She had little time for dreaming, actually, but she was most excellent in her reliable service.

She was a genius at saving money in the market, juggling sales and coupons and price comparisons in her mind like a master mathematician. She was a whiz in the kitchen, could serve up seven dishes perfectly timed and piping hot all at the right moment—nothing ever burned. She was a whiz at the workplace and wonderful with the children, always whisking them from this educational program to that. She never stood up a friend, was always five minutes early. All her bills were paid in advance. Every six months, she faithfully made it to the dentist.

One day, this girl felt a little rumbling in her tummy. Bread. She realized she was hungry for a bit of bread. Glancing hurriedly at her watch, she calculated that she would be late for her next meeting if she stopped for bread, and she couldn't have that! "Bread!" cried her belly. "Shush!" cried her planner.

To her humiliation, all through the meeting, her stomach kept up the protest. It growled and it gurgled; it produced all manner of unsophisticated sounds. On it grumbled, louder and louder like a big angry cat. The woman thought about excusing herself from the meeting to feed the persnickety feline, but she didn't want to disappoint anyone with her absence, so on she sat and took diligent, copious notes.

Alas! The meeting ran long and she had no choice but to rush from there to the store to pick up her order before it closed. On the way, a baker stood outside his shop offering samples and the smells beckoned her, pulled her, slapped her in the nose, but she turned the other cheek and walked on.

Later, at the next meeting, there were pastries sitting out for attendees. Her stomach looked at the generous platters and saw relief, but the mathematician in her brain was already busy counting calories—oy! You really shouldn't!—and by sheer willpower she pulled herself away from the extra hip fat lurking so deceptively in the succulent desserts. Intimidated by her self-control, women all around the room cut back on their own portions lest they look like pigs . . . which is how, unbeknownst to her, the meeting host far overpaid for catering that didn't get eaten.

Finally, at half past seven, it was time to go home after a long day's work, but as she headed down the long hallway that led to the parking lot, she began to feel a little wobbly. Her legs began to shake; her head went dizzy. Darkness seemed to be overtaking her vision; her mouth went dry and she felt nauseated. She reached out her hands to steady herself, but it was too late. Down she dropped, passed out from hunger. When the paramedics arrived, they asked her what she had eaten that day, but she couldn't remember. There had been no time for breakfast, no time for lunch either, and obviously she hadn't yet made it home for dinner . . . .

"What did you eat yesterday then?" they asked. She found she couldn't remember that either. Embarrassed, she went red in the face. Surely she had eaten something! Why couldn't she remember? Behind her, the Employee of the Month poster gleamed on the wall, her straight white teeth stretched wide in a perfectly photogenic smile.

The end.

There are those who refuse to work for their bread and there are those who refuse their bread by working. We cannot speak honestly about the sin of idleness unless we speak of both kinds. Idleness is not always sitting on your bum—though it can be that. Idleness is doing that which keeps you from doing what you are meant to do. Idleness is any form of wasted energy. Idleness is abusing the clock rather than honoring it, trying to coerce time to meet your demands rather than opening time patiently like the gift it was designed to be. The author of 2 Thessalonians speaks of idlers and busybodies, and they are one and the same.

Eugene Peterson says there are two reasons for being busy. One is being busy because we are vain; we want to look important. The other reason for being busy is that we are lazy; we indolently let others decide what we will do instead of resolutely deciding for ourselves. We don't put forth the necessary effort to refuse what we need to refuse. In other words, busyness is not a virtue, whichever way you slice it.[2]

Idleness is a failure of discernment. It is not paying attention to what you most need to do. It is spinning your wheels rather than moving forward; it is lots of activity and very little meaning. Idleness is believing you *must* earn your bread but never eat it. The opposite of idleness is recognizing that *all* your bread is a gift to you, and then breaking out in spontaneous acts of gratitude, stuffing your face and cutting up slices for your friends.

Idleness is what we do when we believe in scarcity and lack: we twiddle our thumbs or we obsess in worry or we imagine five hundred energy-draining ways to fix things or we engage in aggressive competition against our neighbor because what else can be done when there isn't enough to go around?

Too often we act out of fear: our fear of failing, fear of losing, fear of disappointing. This is an idle waste of our energies. By contrast, a belief in abundance and a trust that there is enough—that we are enough—opens the way for right participation and meaningful action in the world. Good work always arises out of love, and love is abundance.

Idleness is the inertia that keeps us from loving well. It is less a laziness of body than a laziness of spirit, a wilting of our courage.

Love, after all, is a frightening endeavor. Some people keep really busy so as not to remember that they have forgotten to be brave.

Clarissa Pinkola Estés writes, "The poor ego is always looking for an easy way out. Deep in the wintry parts of our minds, we are hardy stock and know there is no such thing as a work-free transformation. We know that we will have to burn to the ground in one way or another, and then sit right in the ashes of who we once thought we were and go on from there. But another side of our natures, a part more desirous of languor, hopes it won't be so, hopes the hard work can cease so slumber can resume."[3]

What is your true work? Whatever it is, it will take courage, and it will likely take time.

Patience is on the opposite end of the spectrum from idleness. Scurry is often a sign that we are guilty of the sin of sloth, that we are *avoiding* our *real work*, that we are indulging our impatience and our fretting rather than feeding the stomach of our trust. When you are not being idle, the belly of your soul is slightly bulging, full of nutrition, of daily bread, of the nourishment meant for you and not the nourishment meant for another.

This is key: distinguishing your work from the work of others—knowing the work that is meant for you keeps you humble, keeps your ego quiet, saves you from the exhaustion of comparison, and fires you up with a sense of calling that is all your own. Only you can learn your lessons, do your work, intake your meal. Trying to live off another's scraps of insight and dedication and depth will get you nowhere. To siphon off another's fuel will feel to your soul like gnawing on an empty wooden fork, like gulping down a glass of air. Don't try to borrow from what others have achieved. Do the work you are meant to do. Attend to your stomach when it is hungry. Give thanks for your food. Sleep when you are tired. Work hard when you are called. Rather than earning your bread, honor your bread by doing the work set before you. Once you know what to do, don't run away and don't hide. Once you reach the chasm between your dreams and reality, don't turn back. Leap.

And the God who called you will be abundantly faithful, will bring you to completion, will catch you when you jump or recreate you with wings. Amen.

3

voice:
risk in preaching

αfτεR mɣ ɔɪʋoRce, I was working with a healer and she encouraged me to join her in making sounds—*ya-ohm, la-ohm, ta-ohm*. I could not seem to do it. Try as I might, my throat felt constricted. I felt like the shy girl at a junior high dance hiding in the shadows, unable to move, much less dance. After a few feeble attempts, I gave up and listened to her voice in silence. I felt angry at my inability, at my discomfort, at my unbreakable reserve. In my frustration, the thought came to me, "I am one without a voice. I am noiseless." After the session, I shared this self-description with my healer friend and she said, "Ah, yes, you couldn't even say, 'ohm.'"

Damn. What is wrong with me? I can't emit a simple sound?! Why can't I speak?

I don't have many nightmares when I sleep, but when I do, I am nearly always unable to make a sound. If I can speak, then I am unable to move or to make lights come on. In other words, I seem to be most afraid of my inability to take positive action on account of my own well-being. In real life, instead of conquering this fear and opening my mouth, I often get mad instead at the people who talk loudly or who do not listen, as if it were their fault that I am frozen, that my words are stuck in my throat like thick milkshake in a straw. It has been a long labor to find my voice.

I think voice is the hardest thing to attain because it cannot be imitated, learned, or rushed. It must sprout from within, sometimes at an aggravatingly slow pace, and many obstacles will thwart its growth.

Voice is also one of the most important things to attain because without it you are just one more talker among the masses—the masses where everybody jabbers and nearly no one listens. Your task is to find and use your voice, because you are the *only one* who can do that job. Anybody can copycat other voices. Only you can wake up your own and find the thing you're meant to say.

Too many of us constantly move our mouths, but so little sound is coming out. Of course, I am meaning so little *powerful* sound, sound with waves that can slam into dams and crack them open.

Without even trying, we all make peeps and squeaks or blow smoke. We all can wax long and grand, chasing circles, and we all contribute in one way or another to the murderous polarization that is poisoning country and home. This is not the kind of sound I am referring to. We need no more of the slick, slanderous, slippery words that mark this day and time, which is one of the reasons I am a huge advocate of *more silence.*

Also, more listening. So many of us need to shut our mouths and listen, but we've lost this art and replaced it with bullying, ignorance, and arrogance. Do not speak until you have *heard* something worth repeating and resaying in your own way, and understand that it takes a while to discern what is worthwhile and what is not. But eventually, out from the silence and out from the listening, your voice *must* emerge because it is the one unique gift you have to give. No one else has your voice.

Unfortunately, the world is not going to wait around until you *feel* ready. You will inevitably be forced to speak things before you are certain. If you are quaking in your boots right before you open your mouth, that is a good sign. It means you have exited the ignorance and arrogance and bullying of our culture and entered sacred ground. Your shoes are shaking because you're meant to take them off. Your truest voice is a burning bush that you're afraid to touch. Once you're scared shitless, you're on the right track. You may not be there yet, but you are pointed in the right direction.

A few months ago I began reading my poetry at a local open-mic poetry reading. I found that I was reading every poem as if it were an apology—my voice growing especially soft right when I got to my favorite lines or the most powerful words—as if I were embarrassed of my own thoughts and opinions. The leader of the group kept telling me, "Project! You have something to say and we need to hear it. Project!"

This pissed me off. "I can't help it! This soft voice, it is the only voice I have!" I wanted to say/shout back at him, but of course I just smiled politely, nodded knowingly, agreed to try harder, and kept right on whispering my poems.

Finally, I was fed up with his constant prodding and determined to write a poem about my frustration. I titled it "Quiet," and it began with the lines,

Why is everything I say . . .
a suggestion?
Why does my voice get tinier
when it has something to say?

On and on I wrote, exploring the source of my reserve until I got to the bottom of it. Once I was finished writing, I memorized the poem and then forced myself to belt it out at the next open mic. I brought friends for support because I wasn't sure I could do it. It took all my nerve to read loudly and boldly, but when I did, the room changed. People listened. People applauded. People *heard* me.

It can be hard to grow enough to use your voice. I used to be terrified of ever saying anything publically about my feminism. I was worried what people would think of me. I was afraid of further rocking the boat. (Wasn't it enough that I was a female pastor in a male-dominated denomination? Wouldn't it be *too much* if people knew I was a full-fledged feminist?) Once I began to speak out about my passion for the equality of women, to truly express what was in my heart, I found that people—especially women, but men too—started coming out of the woodwork, resonating with my words and sharing their own. *We crave hearing the words that are in our hearts, and we need people who will speak them for us and show us the way.* The deep, private struggles that keep us feeling isolated and alien are often the very struggles that are universal if we would only risk letting that inner battle be seen and heard.

Finding our voice requires risk. We do not learn how to trust the Holy Spirit and the spark of the divine that resides within us by gritting our teeth and *trying* to have faith. We cultivate trust by moving our bodies, opening our mouths, and taking action that requires a leap into the safety net of God and will eventually prove to us that the net can hold.

This feels like freefalling, and first you will pray, "Help!" and think that you are flailing out of control. Next you will pray, "Wow! Look at this view," and you will know gratitude.

In terms of your voice, do not settle for anything counterfeit, or you will deeply disappoint yourself. If your growth ever seems to reach a stalemate, examine whether you are taking regular, reasonable risks. If not, take a risk ASAP. It doesn't matter much what kind, as long as you do not abandon your integrity to do it. Active risk-taking is the only way to learn and change. Dawna Markova writes, "There is something highly passionate about living in conscious relationship to fear. I have been practicing daily by venturing into the unknown and risking a reach . . . . These little practices with risk and reach, fear and promise at my edge give me daily shots of vitality."[4]

I once had a dream where I was chased by a big werewolf through a large, rickety house. I ran up the stairs to an attic space to hide. I knew the werewolf would find me; I had no doubts I would be discovered. My entire strategy was to hide well enough so that by the time the werewolf found me, he would have already turned back into a man, and I would be safe. I would *survive* danger by silently hiding.

But then I noticed that I was standing next to a large window, and it occurred to me that I could jump, that I had another option. I was several stories up, so jumping was a risk. I might injure myself, but I would also have the whole outdoors to keep running, to escape. I was standing by the pane of glass, weighing my options, knowing the wolf would arrive any moment, when I woke up.

This dream arrived at one of the most critical moments in my life, when I had to make some hugely important decisions. It was as if the dream was describing my crossroads, and I woke when I did because I had yet to make the choice. I sensed that my life was calling to me, begging me to come out from hiding and take a leap.

But when I shared this dream with a friend and described the two options the dream had given me, she had another perspective. She pointed out that the dream wasn't over yet, and that all kinds of things could still happen. It wasn't just hide or jump. "You could sprout wings," she suggested with a sparkle in her eye. "Or maybe you turn around to face the wolf and turn into a dragon. Keep dreaming."

One day I decided to write an ending to this dream in my journal. I had no idea how I was going to end it, but what came to me as I wrote was that I turned to face the werewolf and I began to sing. (*How is this supposed to help?* my inner critic complained to my inner storyteller.) But my voice was strong and loud, and the melody was haunting and fierce. My voice rang out across the landscape, and creatures from all across the land flew to my aid at the sound of it.

A few months later I had another dream where evil men came to break up a wedding celebration I was officiating, with plans to do great violence among the guests. They forced me to stand in front of everyone and read from a letter I had written for the bride and groom. They intended my reading to be a mockery, a humiliation to the crowd who now feared for their lives. But though I was inwardly shaking, I read my letter with conviction and confidence, and the words were so beautiful that it moved all the people to tears, even the perpetrators, and the terrible violence they had planned was thwarted. I woke up feeling the power of my own voice.

If you are a hider, trying to escape life's dangers with your silence and avoidance, then start talking, even if you have to begin with mouse-sized squeaks. If you have been a shouter, that is, one who speaks in a voice that is not your own, start getting quiet, and try not to open your mouth again until you have found your stillness.

Everything that is not your authentic voice is defined by fear and insecurity. Your real voice will be a fearful thing to raise; you will quake when you do it. But you will be using your voice *in spite* of your fear, not as a tool controlled by your fear. This is the difference—whether you are being coerced by the fear or whether the fear is being told off by your courage. There is no simply eradicating the feeling of fear. Like it or not, risk is required.

Special note to the faint of heart: If you are a big chicken like me for whom any kind of gamble threatens to undo you, I empathize wholeheartedly. Even so, you *must* come undone. Start small if that is what it takes. Do one brave thing a day, however tiny. Or, if you can't manage that quite yet, make a list of all the brave things you have *already* done. Anything counts as long as it scares you—be it petting a dog or visiting the dentist (I didn't say you had to share this list with anyone). I promise that you will be amazed at how brave you *already* are. Then think about adding one more tiny thing to the list *today*. It will feel exhilarating if you do, and every step, no matter how small, takes you closer to finding your voice.

Stone Bellowing Truth

Luke 19:28-40 (Palm Sunday,
Covenant Baptist Church)

In Genesis 4, when Cain kills his brother Abel, God approaches
Cain about the coldhearted murder. Cain says, "Am I my brother's
keeper?" God replies, "Listen!"

Listen:
your brother's blood
cries out
(to me!)
from the *ground*
the ground which gaped
wide its mouth
to swallow the blood of your brother
which dripped from your hands[5]
your brother is dead
but his blood still lives
and cries and moans
with the earth as its witness
you thought you were alone
but the dirt and the trees saw
and heard and smelled and tasted
and with blood still on its tongue
the ground whispered your secrets
to my ear and I am here
to call you to account

It was not what Cain expected. He had committed a hidden
crime; he wasn't supposed to get caught. Besides, in his private
thoughts he had quite thoroughly justified his deeds—never would

he have been provoked to such anger had it not been for the extreme unfairness that had wounded his pride. He was a good, decent, hard-working man, after all.

We do not get to hear Abel's side of things, for he was dead before a word from his mouth could be recorded or heard, but the very dust of the earth woke up to tell his story in the ear of God, and this is the part Cain did not anticipate or plan for: that Abel's lifeblood would continue to speak, even after Cain thought he had shut it down.

But apparently, despite the recent curse of the earth, God's creation was still fundamentally good and operating in league with its Creator, telling God the things it saw, crying loudly on behalf of the wronged, begging God to intervene and set things right.

The vision of a nonhuman voice crying out on behalf of justice—in this case, blood and dirt —is one of the most profoundly moving images for me in all of Scripture. A similar theme shows up in Habakkuk 2. The prophet is exposing the injustices that pervade the lives of the people, and he says,

> Woe to him who builds his house
> by unjust gain,
> setting his nest on high
> to escape the clutches of ruin!
> You have plotted the ruin
> of many peoples,
> shaming your own house,
> forfeiting your own life.
> The stones of the wall
> will cry out,
> and the beams of the woodwork
> will echo it.[6]

In this instance, those who build houses by unjust gain will experience the very building materials of their homes turning against them! The stones will cry; the beams will echo them. Inanimate objects will be provoked if the people do not maintain justice. One gets the eerie sense that an underlying current of truth and justice is at work in the world to restore all things, a current that cannot be silenced, for this is God's world. No matter who thwarts the way of truth and justice and kindness, some*thing* will rise up in dissent, because God created a world that cannot be mute in the face of injustice. When human beings fall silent, other voices will come out from the woodwork to speak the truth, to decry the cruelty and oppression. Stones, wood, dirt, blood—all around us the earth erupts in protest. We may remain as deaf and oblivious as Cain, but God hears every sound, and when the earth rages, the heavens are moved.

Now in today's story, Jesus rides in on a donkey—which, by the way, in biblical lore is an animal known to speak up when needed. Anyway, Jesus rides in on a donkey, perhaps to fulfill prophecy or perhaps simply as a way to say to the downtrodden and the oppressed who pressed in around him, "I belong with you." He rode in on a lowly donkey so the lowly would know, here's a guy who wants to be with us. These were the people without a voice, the silenced, the shushed, the hungry, and the sick. And for one short day in history, their voices rang out loud and clear and defiant, "Hosanna! Hosanna! Blessed is the king who comes in the name of the Lord!" He was their king, and they were proud to proclaim it.

This made the religious leaders a mite uncomfortable. They liked to control who speaks and when, you see. They definitely didn't like the rabble picking new leadership on their own accord, and they didn't want anybody stirring up political trouble when they'd worked so hard to maintain peace with the powers.

"Teacher, rebuke your disciples!"

They tried desperately to regain control, to which Jesus, of course, merely gave a genial wave and a nonsense reply. "I tell you," he said, "if they keep quiet, the stones will cry out."

Jesus heard things that only the gods can hear, that is, the creaking and cracking of the earth under the weight of injustice and violence. If the religious leaders had paid much attention to old Habakkuk, they would have been less perplexed by Jesus' baffling belief in the rocks, but as it was, they scratched their heads and walked away not knowing what Jesus knew: that the people crying "Hosanna! Our King comes!" were not singing a new song but were joining the echo of the wood beams, entering the chorus of the stones and the ground and Abel's blood, adding their voices to the choir that has been singing the truth since the beginning of time.

And it is on the wave of this melody that Jesus will dismount his donkey, stride into the temple, and drive out the moneychangers—one of the few recorded acts that display Jesus' righteous anger. I imagine he walked into that place with the sounds of his people and the songs of the stones reverberating in his ears, begging him to set things right and confront every Cain.

There is an infectious energy to the palm procession and the temple purging that feels like it cannot be stopped. The people have found their voices; their leader has unleashed his fervor. The next thing that happens is Jesus starts teaching in the temple every day, and the chief priests and leaders try to kill him, but "they could not find any way to do it, because all the people hung on his words."[7] There's no stopping him, no shutting down the people who follow him, no silencing of the stones. Only those of us who know the rest of the story know to feel a little wary of all this raging success.

Palm Sunday is that odd celebratory moment that pitches us headlong into passion week. In less than a week, the tables will have turned entirely . . . .

As soon as Jesus gets captured by the soldiers and stands his trial, the adoring crowd will go back to being who they were before: silenced slaves without a voice. Perhaps they will protest his death in their own subtle ways, like the women who follow Jesus all the way to the hill with tears in their eyes, beating their breasts, or the two Marys who will not leave his side, following him even to the tomb. But by and large, the only voices that ring out on that fateful Friday are the ones shouting, "Crucify, crucify!" Imagine the horror of the Hosanna-crying crowd as they watched their dreams slipping away. They did not know how to fight back, how to speak up, and the words that rang out around them—"Crucify, crucify!"—dropped like lead in their stomachs and drowned out their hopes and filled them with dread, and they wept and wept until their Savior was dead, salvation no more, with despair in its stead.

It is a gut-wrenching turn of events when the celebrated Savior with the gumption to purge the temple ends up beaten and bruised and silenced, just like the silenced ones he'd come to care for. It must have seemed to the people like the very end of all their hopes, a complete and total loss. He hung from that tree and the world fell silent, the people struck mute in terror and disbelief and loss . . . . Yet not all was quiet.

In the Gospel of Matthew, when Jesus breathes his last, the earth shakes and the rocks split. Having been around for ages, the stones could sense that even now, in the darkest hour, Jesus was altering the course of things. He wasn't giving in or giving up; he was giving himself into the suffering, entering death freely in audacious solidarity with the broken. Was the earth opening that day in order to receive the blood of our Savior as it mixed with the spilt blood of all the Abels before him? It was a dark and terrible hour indeed, but the earth knew it couldn't possibly be the end, could it? Were the rocks splitting in agony or in protest or both? Did they emit a terrible sound when they cracked? Could God the Father stand to listen, or did God's own voice join the wail?

We hail Jesus as the supreme example to follow, but really, what he did was an act we could never follow. He took on the pain of the world, let them kill him, and then he came back living, and I can't even make it so far as to handle my pain and forgive my enemies, much less die and come back. Which is why I wave palm branches this day to hail him as my king, because here is a man who comes among us, comfortable in the presence of average folks like us, but unafraid to suffer and forgive, die a criminal's death, and then live. I don't know if I could ever be like him, but praise God he became like us, human and hurting, to share in our suffering and redeem all pain.

Sometimes we are the desperate Hosanna criers, you and I, joining the groan of the earth that waits for the world to be made right and seeing in a poor carpenter boy from Nazareth the making of a king. Sometimes we are more like the religious leaders, a bit put out by Jesus' strange success and the threat he poses to our security and our way of seeing the world, and without even meaning to, we try to crucify him out of the picture. Some way or another, we are part of this story every Lent and every Easter, and only the Spirit of God can discern which crowd defines us this time around.

Though what I *really* find myself wondering is, what would a choir of rocks sound like, anyway? Would they have a gravelly sound, or would they make a smooth, melodious ripple? Did it even matter if they could hit the right notes, or was any noise at all enough to catch the notice of God?

This year, when I read the story, I find myself identifying with the stones. I want to be like a rock who stubbornly sings, however off-key the notes, however bland my stories, however pervasive my lisp. I want to be the one who finds a thousand new ways to speak, to tell the one nugget of truth that's been entrusted to me, however inadequately I may say it. My part will never sound perfect because it is only part of the larger whole, but without my part the world will miss something crucial, and so I must find a way to tell it and tell it boldly, the part of God's righteous truth entrusted to me. I must find a way to let it shine. Whether anyone hears me or not, I want to know I joined the chorus with heart and soul. I want to sing for those without a voice, calling out to God on their behalf, joining the great choir of justice that sings on and on and on . . . .

"Hosanna! Blessed is the King!" Amen.

Women, We Are Bent

Luke 13:10-17 (Covenant Baptist Church)

There are many women who are bent and who stay bent. Forgive me, men, I'm less familiar with your chronic ailments, and I would feel like an arrogant fool if I hazarded a guess, but this *bentness*—this eighteen-year-long bentness—is a sickness I understand intimately. And I can assure you, it is no coincidence at all in the story that she is a woman.

Women take a long time to learn how to stand tall, how to square our shoulders, how to lift our chins, how to take up our space. Whether it was society or family dynamics or misguided theology or sustained abuse or our own unrelenting insecurity, we were trained or have trained ourselves to remain stooped, and like those earlier women who bound their feet to keep themselves small, we have stayed bound and we have stayed small, and the only payoff is that we cannot run anymore.

We work until we are bone-tired, and we nod and smile politely until we no longer know what a real smile feels like, much less a real yes. We scurry to please and to pat and to pamper until we've puttered our lives away and tuned out the song of our souls.

We are bent. As women we live hunched-over lives underneath the weight of demands and expectations and comparisons and the need to be perfect and the longing to be pretty or, if not pretty, at least somewhat appealing, the right kind of mother or lover or daughter, to get it all right and to make the rightness appear effortless, to be both gracious and gifted, gorgeous but not aware of it, glamorous without trying or seeming like you're trying, to be a great cook and skilled at décor and excellent with babies and smart (but don't show off your smartness!) and . . . and . . . and . . . .

These burdens bend us into a half-life—it is like we are walking through life looking down at the ground. Spine cracked over, we're not able to look up and out and around and *see* the world and our place in it because we've got our noses to the grindstone. We are bent.

It is no coincidence or surprise that when Jesus meets a woman, she is a hunched-over woman. He had been encountering hunched-over women all his life, no doubt, but finally, here is a woman who *knows* she is bent and wishes to straighten.

While the male theologians have told us the sin of man is pride, the female theologians have remarked that the sin of woman is lack of pride, and for bent-over women, this is true. The poison that keeps a woman small is the failure to know her worth. The lack of faith to know that she has a place in this world, that there is a space here meant to be occupied by her. It takes the good kind of pride to stretch out your limbs and take up your space.

Women are taught instead to step aside, to squeeze into the last inch of the elevator corner to make room for others, to hide themselves from view, to shine the spotlight elsewhere, to retreat to the sink and dishes on cue when conversation takes a certain turn.

There is certainly something to be said for selfless service and self-sacrificing surrender, and where would the world be if it were not for the silent patience of our spiritual mothers? But there is a difference between giving of yourself because you choose to and giving of yourself because you don't know what else to do, what else you *can* do.

There's a difference between standing tall, doing good and noble work, and crouching over, spending all your energy watching where you go because you are afraid of stepping on someone's toes. It's not real service—not the kind that matters—if we're just shuffling among bigger people, being cautious not to offend. To serve the world is to get big yourself and be in it as a real player.

Coach Jim used to tell us on the basketball court, "Get big!" I can hear his voice now, always saying the same two things. First, sounding slightly annoyed, "Bounce pass!" (something we could never seem to remember) and "Get big!" which, as an exceptionally and irreparably small person, I took offense at. Occasionally I even felt like shouting back at him, "I can't get big! Look at me! Give me a pointer I can actually follow."

But he just kept saying the same blasted thing: "Bounce pass! Get big!" Of course, the real purpose of playing sports is to get simple ideas through thick heads. Eventually I learned that a pass *around* my defender's arms was statistically more successful than all the passes I kept attempting *through* their arms.

And I figured out that "Get big" had nothing to do with literal size. It meant *take up your space.* Be a force to be reckoned with. Spindly appendages and all, *show off* your fierceness. Be imposing. Stretch. Fill your area. Loom over the ball as it approaches. Get in the way of the offense.

Make your body *say something.* Say, "I'm not backing down" *with your body.* Say, "You can't get by me" with your legs. Say, "I am after that ball" with your arms. Say to your opponent, "I am ready to face you" with the large look in your eye. Speak! Get big! Play ball!

Women, we are bent.

I wish I knew what to tell the men about a Bible story like this one, but I don't, except to say thank you to the ones like Jim who encouraged me not only on the court but also later to go ahead and take up my space and not apologize. Thank you to those who've been the hands and feet of Jesus walking among women and lifting our heads. Thank you to men who have made it stop— the pushing down and the silencing of women.

After a long, long, long ailment, you are helping to heal us, and in being healers, you are being healed too. We are healing one another, don't you see?

Tragically, religion gets misused time and again to keep women down, but, of course, what matters more is that Jesus raises women up and tells them to stand, to walk, to go, to sin no more.

Leaders of synagogues and churches get indignant to see this work Jesus is doing among women, setting them free from the evil spirit that keeps them bound and crippled.

In the story, it is lunacy that the religious leaders would prevent someone being set free on the Sabbath. What else is the Sabbath for if not to liberate the captive from evil? It is lunacy to resist, but the letter of the law has crippled these leaders, bent them away from the Spirit of God (*"Whatever you do, Jesus, don't set a woman loose on the Sabbath!"*). Unlike the woman, they do not wish to stand tall and look out and see what God is really up to in the world.

But all this deters Jesus not. "Ought not this woman be set free?" he replies. It is hard to argue with Jesus

This miracle once got a whole crowd to its feet, rejoicing at the wonderful things Jesus does.

We were bent and now we are free.

Hallelujah. Amen.

4

skin:
vulnerability in preaching

As i sat in an abbey in Oregon, listening to the monks sing-pray, a piece of me cracked open and I began to cry. It had been nearly a full year since I had experienced a strong sense of God's presence. I had observed the Divine carrying me through a year of grief in all manner of indirect ways—through poetry, through friends, through nature, etc.—but the closeness I used to feel to the *person* of Jesus had been missing for quite some time. Letting the tears run down my cheeks that lonely night in the abbey, I felt how much I missed him. I was grieved by the loss.

That same year, in addition to Jesus' seeming disappearance, I was surviving the rapid disintegration of my marriage. I was enduring undeserved slander from a few people I used to trust, being harassed by an emotionally unstable person, and bearing the weight of financial strain. It was a trying year for me, and in the midst of it God was oh so silent.

When I first entered this particular season of spiritual upheaval and felt the undeniable absence of God's direct voice and the sudden paralyzed muteness of my own prayers, I worried that I was turning into a fraud.

How can I preach every single Sunday while living in this void? I feel so removed from the God of my sermons. How can I talk so freely of Jesus when I can no longer talk freely to him on a daily basis? Won't this make me a fake?

My sermon-writing process ground to a halt. I felt frozen. But, of course, time did not freeze at all, and Sunday came every week, as reliably as the sunrise. And somehow—I can't even explain it to you—by Sunday morning I had a sermon, and more than that, I had a sermon that didn't feel like a lie.

For months I struggled painfully with every single sermon, convinced it wouldn't materialize in time for Sunday. I could have allowed myself to feel totally defeated and inadequate—and there were plenty of lonely hours when I felt that way. But on the whole, I chose to accept my process. I chose to accept God's silence as well as my silence toward God. I chose to accept each sermon that arose (often at the last minute after much unproductive agonizing) as absolute Grace and Miracle. I chose to find small ways to be appropriately honest and transparent about my struggle without letting my inner battle dominate what happened in or out of church. I chose to let things unfold in their own way, in their own time. I chose to accept doubt as a sign of faith, because those who doubt and struggle are *connected somehow* to God or else we wouldn't feel the ache. I chose to be grateful for any bit of Grace I was able to see, however small it appeared.

Learning how to be authentically and tastefully vulnerable as a minister, as a preacher, as a *person* is hard and slow-going work. Someone recently asked me if I would like to lead a workshop on vulnerability and transparency, and so far I've declined because I do not know where to begin to teach *how* to do it. All I know is how it worked for me: I came to a point in my life where my personal life was being ravaged by grief and relational upheaval, and I was forced to make a choice: get vulnerable or die on the inside.

Sitting with my tears in that abbey was the first time after a year of struggle that I truly understood that, while my *preference* would be to preach and minister out of my deep, abiding sense of God's personal love for me, there was *nothing wrong* with ministering and preaching out of my doubt, brokenness, and longing. It was, in fact, a deeply honest way to minister (and I'd been worrying that I was a fraud!). I was also given the sense that I was not going to be ministering out of the emptiness forever, that I would someday *feel* connected to the personal element of the Divine, and that I would be okay in all phases—preaching out of longing for God and preaching out of the fullness of God and even preaching out of the indifference toward God that sometimes hits us all. As long as I was speaking truth, wrestling honestly, exposing my heart, and doggedly showing up, then I was preaching with sincerity, and that was always an opening for God to join the act and make it meaningful.

Preaching is like a little act of incarnation, and while that sounds mystical and sacramental, incarnational preaching *feels like* the holy just put on skin and took on body odor, a beer gut full of human fears, and a little bit of flab in all the wrong places. Incarnation feels far removed from glorious—think stinky manger in a dingy stable with the uterine goo staining the hay, and you can see what I mean. This may be the messiest bit of preaching: letting our humanness into it and believing that our awkward bodies are, in reality, reflections of the divine image. Letting ourselves *be seen* is the most important (and maybe the only) way in which we do any real *leading* in a congregation. It is how we teach people to be church—not by fixing their brokenness like heroes but by letting our brokenness shimmer. We can say, "You are welcome here" as often as we like, but no one will believe that until we show them. We must show by example that you can bring your whole self into the church—your questions, your struggles, and your fears.

The worst thing you can do to a pulpit is use it as a platform to proclaim all you *know* and all you've *figured out* and all the *solutions* you want the congregation to take from your palm like candy.

Some people come to church looking for neatly packaged answers, of course, and they will feel contentedly obliged when you so provide. All the while, you remain alien to them, and they remain alien to their true souls. The pulpit is best used for splitting open and getting to what is real—the realness of being human, the realness of God in all God's mystery and evasiveness, the realness of community holding on to each other by fraying threads, the realness of beauty amid disappointments.

To me, the two most captivating bits of the Christian faith are incarnation and resurrection: God in human flesh and death defeated.

But these truths *must be embodied* if they are to be made real in this age for this people. That is, we must be willing to *live them*, to allow God to be incarnate through us and to let things die that they might be revived. Unfortunately, the church often goes to great lengths to *avoid* incarnation and resurrection. God-with-us is too messy, and the death that must come first is too high a price to pay for resurrection.

The apostle Paul writes that we are "always carrying in the body the death of Jesus, so that the life of Jesus may also be made visible in our bodies."[8] What can that possibly mean? I think it is part mystery, part pain. It doesn't mean we become martyrs who seek hurt, but it does mean that we let the hurt we see into our hearts. Rather than shielding ourselves from the heartache of reality, we carry deaths and disappointments within us. Sometimes the church presents a safe, sanitized religion that doesn't get mixed up with the complications of living and the pains of dying. But this sort of compartmentalized faith, separate from real life and the horrors we see around us, is increasingly unsatisfactory.

In this generation, we are hungry for incarnation—God with us in the thick of it—and hungry for resurrection—the possibility of a hope that takes a lot of hits but never stays dead. This is the religion people desire: not one that denies our humanness but one that takes our humanness fully into account and still finds a way to hold on to hope. It means we do not deny or sugarcoat the gruesomeness of living. We do not pretend that faith eradicates our sour feelings. We admit the absurdity of quick fixes, even in this high-speed era, because we experience a world that remains broken. By refusing to turn a blind eye to how painful this life can be, we reawaken our hunger for a God who will be in the chaos with us and who can grow life from the compost of our hurts.

On a more exciting note, talking honestly is not all gloom and doom and painful awareness. There is, I would say, a tasteful sensuality to vulnerability. We crave the skin-to-skin contact of being our realest selves and encountering the real in others. But we may be timid to initiate that kind of contact. We want others to show their colors, but we are reticent to go first for fear that we will be judged if we let our flabbier parts into the light where we can be seen.

This reluctance can result in exaggerated appetites because we aren't getting our legitimate needs met. For example, the tendency toward narcissism in social media forums is rarely about self-absorption, though it seems that way. It is about the human soul crying out to be seen and heard and validated and not knowing any other way to do it. We over-share in a public forum because we've lost of the art of private conversation. We've lost our avenues for honest dialogue and supportive community. We've lost the nerve to say to a friend face to face, "I feel like I'm losing it," so we rant about traffic and jerks and flu symptoms via the Internet because we lack a healthy way to process daily disappointment. What we really want is someone to hold our hand as we walk through life's scariest terrain, but we settle for stuff that makes us feel held for a moment, though it has little substance.

Rampant promiscuity is the same sort of distraction device as rampant tweeting. Our appetite for connection is so ravenous that we are willing to get in bed with a stranger just to feel alive, because we don't know how to be known by our own friends and neighbors. Being known is what generates life, but we've smothered the capacity for genuine intimacy with the modest garments of perfected appearances, cloaking who we are with the false belief that hiding will keep us safe. So we get naked in all the wrong places, too afraid to let our skin show when we are among the family and friends who will look us in the eye and still be there in the morning.

This is an opportunity for church to be counter to the culture. There is a nakedness to vulnerable preaching that is uncomfortable and scary but absolutely appropriate and needed. When we become vulnerable, we are recovering intimacy from the bondage of legalism and making it good and holy again, and accessible to all. We are acknowledging in front of people that we have bodies and cravings and mistakes and fears, that life is messy and we are human and being human is a fine thing to be. By opening our hearts, we are opening the possibility for connection and friendship. We are obliterating the false choice between prudence and licentiousness and saying that there is a third way. There is an alternative way to live in the world that is neither stuffy nor sordid. There is a way to embody love and truth and grace, a way to integrate our experiences into the life of faith rather than keeping faith in a separate compartment from the real concerns of living.

Consider Mother Mary as a model for vulnerable living. Who else in all of Scripture had her literal body so wrapped up in the life of Jesus? Who else knew the Gospel trials and triumphs as intimately as the mother of the man who bore our sins and carried our sorrows? If anyone knew what Paul meant about "carrying in the body the death of Jesus," it had to be her.

Incarnating the Resurrection
Mother of God how hard was it
for you to watch
what you had labored and birthed
be killed?

We too carry such deaths in our bodies.
Even as we serve as tombs for murdered
dreams, may our wombs stay vibrant,
and our love remain warm. May we shower
the burial grounds with incense
and spice, rising early to sit with what
we have lost. May the grief that meets us
in the morning one day lead to an
emptied-out grave and the music of angels.

The State of Our Union

1 Corinthians 13 (Covenant Baptist Church)

It began on a Saturday. It was the first time I walked our labyrinth, the second time I'd stepped foot on this property. It was love-at-first-sight for me. The morning after my interview with the pastor search team, I wound my way through the labyrinth and tried to pray a prayer of surrender: "Lord, this is a place I want to be, but Thy will be done."

Now here we sit, two years later, and my feelings haven't changed a bit, and my prayer is essentially the same: "Lord, this is a place I want to be. Thy will be done here."

A lot of other stuff has changed, though. We have fewer people now than we did then, for one thing. And most notably for me personally, I've undergone some trauma and a major life transition from married to single. Your lives have changed too—sometimes for the better, but some changes have just been plain hard.

It's been good and it's been ugly, and that's the way life goes most of the time. Let me tell you what I've learned about this church in those two years.

You are a courageous people. You have created a space here where we can be real and vulnerable. I know this because I've been very vulnerable in the last year and you've given me a safe haven to be me. That is a courageous way to be in the world, and not many people choose it. We are more accustomed to putting on performances, judging our neighbor and hiding ourselves in shame, and all too often this falseness happens most in a place like the church.

Frederick Buechner made the comment about Alcoholics Anonymous that an alcoholic can be just about anywhere in this country and know there will be an A.A. meeting nearby where she will find "strangers who are not strangers to help and to heal, to listen to the truth and to tell it." Then he says, "This is what the Body of Christ is"—or it should be.[9]

And yet sometimes in the church we've come to expect a certain sanitized politeness. Instead of finding strangers who are not strangers, in the church you can find people you've known for years turned into strangers, neighbors into aliens. Which might explain why one of my favorite moments as a pastor getting to know someone is the first time they cuss in my presence, because most people are extra careful about language around a preacher, so once you've let loose a curse word in front of me, that's when I know the barrier is down. We are friends and we trust each other enough to say what we think and leave the filter behind. I'm not talking about being inappropriate or letting loose with gossip or forgoing respect and dignity. I just mean that if you are a human in this broken world, then there are times when only a four-letter word will do, and if you cannot speak honestly to a pastor, then why should we bother with religion at all? If this is only a place to cover up, not a place to be real?

I guess it might sound like I'm saying that I know this place is the real deal on account of the language I hear, but what I am really saying is that you are a people of courage because you let people be where they are, and the pastor is no exception—you allow her to be herself too—and that is a rare find in an age when we idolize perfectionism and performance and product. You are a courageous people.

Another thing I have learned about this church: You are a truthful people. You can be trusted. I trust you, as a whole body and as individual people. During my first year at Covenant, I sensed that you could be trusted—you all let off a good vibe. But now I know it. I can trust you. Trust you to care for me and for others. Trust you to be kind. Trust you to extend compassion. Trust you to journey with those in pain. Trust you to speak the truth and to hear the truth with grace. You are a truthful, trustworthy people.

You are a patient people. You don't push or prod or meddle or work yourselves into a fuss. You wait things out. You wait on God. You *refuse* to hurry, and, once again, this is a rare find in an age of fast-paced production like ours. This may seem like the least effective thing we do around here—the waiting, the slowing down, the waiting some more. Not just the silence in the worship service, but the waiting for things to get done, the waiting for people to sign up, the waiting to know what to do next. It can feel like a fine line between intentional contemplation and aimless dawdling. But it is a line we walk with patience and slow-growing wisdom, and it is in walking this line that we encounter again and again the call on our lives to *trust*, to relax into a timing we would not choose for ourselves but that will carry us through all the same, and to accept the pace of our neighbor without judgment. You are a patient people.

Along those lines, you are also a gentle people. Ever so gentle. You're never mean. You're never cruel. You are delicate with the wounded. You have a soft touch when handling pain. Again, I know, because I've been the wounded one. I don't speak as an outside observer; I speak as somebody you have helped to heal. For example, *gentle* may not be the first word that pops into your head when you think of Lynette—we mostly know her as funny and feisty—but in this last year, I have known her tenderness amid my pain, and I think of her as this church's Mama Bear. Likewise, I could name every single one of you by name and beside your name list a way you've shown me gentle care. You are a gentle people.

You are a giving people. I think of sharing with you about my friend who needed help, and you jumped to her aid. I think of Jenny and me raising money for Moldova and, seemingly like magic, we had all we needed and more. I think about Carolyn showing up on my doorstep one morning, dropping off a potted plant to brighten my day, and then, just like that, she was on her way. I think of how I have quietly watched you care for others—bringing dinner when someone is sick, calling to check on each other, refusing to talk badly about one another. You are a giving people.

And you are a loving people. Maybe love is a way to sum up everything else I just said, or maybe love is the name for the heartbeat or the oxygen that fuels us. I have known you to be a loving people. As Scripture says in that familiar passage, "If I speak in the tongues of men or of angels, but do not have love, I am only a resounding gong or a clanging cymbal. If I have the gift of prophecy and can fathom all mysteries and all knowledge, and if I have a faith that can move mountains, but do not have love, I am nothing. If I give all I possess to the poor and give over my body to hardship that I may boast, but do not have love, I gain nothing." Which makes me think the reverse is true too: if you do not speak in the tongues of men and angels, if you do not have the gift of prophecy and cannot fathom all mysteries and all knowledge, if your faith has yet to move any mountains, and if you haven't given enough or suffered enough to brag about it, *but you have love*, maybe that is enough. Maybe love is enough.

And the description of love is this: "Love is patient, love is kind. It does not envy, it does not boast, it is not proud. It does not dishonor others, it is not self-seeking, it is not easily angered, it keeps no record of wrongs. Love does not delight in evil but rejoices with the truth. It always protects, always trusts, always hopes, always perseveres." *You* are a loving people.

You are a courageous people.

You are a truthful people.

You are a patient people.

You are a gentle people.

You are a giving people.

You are a loving people.

And there is nowhere I would rather be than right here with you. I'll just tell you, I don't have a clue why we are shrinking as a church when we are so awesome. I mean that seriously. It doesn't make a lick of sense to me. I also don't know why things in our personal lives and things out in the wider world continue to go wrong. I don't know why we never seem to heal *all* the way, why we keep getting hurt and feeling pain and losing our way and running out of steam, why we can't get everything to line up just so. I don't know.

But I know this: We're getting the important stuff right around here. We are encountering Christ in one another around here. We are sticking up for one another rather imperfectly but beautifully around here. We are holding on to faith—sometimes by a thread and sometimes on behalf of someone else—but we're always holding on around here. We are practicing love and integrity and honesty and forgiveness around here—and that doesn't mean we always get it right, but we keep practicing the same things that we might make possible the incarnation of God in this place.

I've given this a lot of thought and prayer, and I'm certainly no expert, but I do not think there is some big thing we are missing, some strategy we need to put in motion or some new concept we need to adopt. I think we are right on track to wherever it is we are going. And no, it's not a worry to me that the destination is a little unclear. I imagine the disciples felt that way nearly all the time.

Mother Teresa once said, "God does not require us to be successful, only that we be faithful." It seems to me that we may never be "successful" by the world's standards, or even by the average church's standards, but that was never the real point, was it? I recently heard a Jesuit priest who does gang intervention in Los Angeles comment that while there is nothing wrong with wanting to be effective, it cannot be the machine that drives us. We are better off "the more we stay anchored in our own fidelity, rather than outcomes."[10] That sounds absolutely right to me: to dive in to our own fidelity.

Here we are, back once again at a New Beginnings Sunday.* For me personally that carries a lot of weight and significance this time around. This year is truly a New Beginning. And in many ways, things are changing and will continue to change. But the good stuff is here to stay, and the call on our lives this year is to dive in to what we already have. To dive in to our fidelity. To give thanks for these blessings and to strive to be good stewards of them. To continue walking the path we are already on, to see the good God has already enacted, and to embrace with abandon the Great Love that is already ours. Amen.

* The start of the new Sunday school year in August.

That Time I Stopped Praying

Luke 11:1-13 (Covenant Baptist Church)

I believe that I emerged from the womb a pray-er—at least, I do not recall a time in my life in which I was not someone who prayed. I have always talked to God, and I don't just mean obligatory mealtime prayers and church prayers. I've always been a person who converses with God, and I don't think anyone taught me or prompted me in this direction so much as the impetus to talk to God was simply there, inside me, like I was born with a cord that stretched from me to heaven, and I had the natural curiosity to tug on it.

Over the years my prayer life has evolved. Since childhood I have been someone who wrote private prayers on paper, having always loved words, but imagine my delight as an adult to discover that some people actually utilize written prayers in public, in corporate worship, and not just in the privacy of their bedrooms and prayer closets. I learned that the beauty of language had a place in the church setting, which was brand-new news to me! I thought all church prayers had to be freewheeling and off-the-cuff to be counted sincere. To find out that written prayers—my most favorite and authentic prayers—could also belong within the community of faith was a wonderful discovery. That was one evolution.

Another evolution was my love for the outdoors. I didn't grow up in a particularly outdoorsy family. We never went camping, so I didn't quite get the picture that I was a nature girl until I was older. But even as a teenager, I was always taking advantage of the early morning hour at church camp—rising before the others, sneaking away to a secluded spot beneath the trees, meeting with God. By college I was sneaking off to the side of the lake, finding God at the water's edge. By seminary, I finally figured out that if I had to be inside to pray, it didn't make sense to be anywhere else except perched by the window, looking out.

This was another evolution—coming to understand that the outdoors was my best space to pray, that nature, for me, was like a lifeline to the Divine.

Yet another evolution was my introduction to Centering Prayer, which was less of an introduction and more of a slow-growing acquaintance with the kind of prayer that uses no words or uses only a single word. I am learning to relinquish and surrender my bustling thoughts, to move into a deeper silence. Centering Prayer is an invitation to God to reorder my heart and soul beyond the level where words can help. This kind of prayer taught me, over time, how to be gentle and gracious to myself at last. By practicing surrender in this way, I started to believe in grace for real, for me. Particularly as I learned to surrender my need to control my prayers and dictate their success, I became more open to the genuine surprise of grace.

Those are just some of the evolutions my prayer life has undergone, and there were others—some arriving like a breath of fresh air into a suffocating practice, others arriving like aggravating frustrations upsetting my status quo. I encountered the rhythms of hourly prayer, and I understood at last the value of repetition. I explored the idea of bodily prayer—walking while praying, or maybe kneeling, for example. I discovered the power of praying with friends and the potency of praying in solitude. I prayed desperate prayers through agonizing seasons of spiritual drought. I also prayed my heart out for someone to live, and then I watched him die.

It is a love-hate relationship we form with prayer if we choose to go on praying even when prayers seem to fail us. We are bound to love-hate prayer, to go through ebbs and flows with it, to experience rising doubts and rising faith, to wind in and then out of comfort and discomfort, the sense of security and the sense of losing our equilibrium, clarity and mystery, disappointment and delight.

Here is my most recent prayer-life evolution. Around the end of November, I stopped praying. That is, I stopped praying in the traditional sense. I couldn't do it anymore. There arose a huge mental and emotional block when I tried to address God. I could not get those two words I'd used thousands of time onto the page—"Dear God." I couldn't say it; I could not speak directly to God.

I started to worry myself a little because I've always told myself I would never be a fraud as a pastor, and I can't imagine a more fraudulent way to pastor than to be a pastor who doesn't pray. I would quit my job before I'd let myself be a fake. And here I was, less than two years into my first pastorate, and all my prayers were stuck in the back of my throat. Frozen there.

But despite the initial panic, I felt an odd peace about the whole affair, like I was going to be okay, my spirit was going to be okay, my pastoring was going to be okay. And so I let myself stop praying. This sounds odd, but it was a deeply spiritual choice. I was saying to God, "I don't know how to reach You anymore, so I want you to reach me instead," and I was half-trusting, half-fearing it would work.

For quite some time all seemed quiet. God was quiet. I was quiet. And then, shyly, slowly, I began to pick up on all the non-verbal communication happening between us, as well as the things I was saying and writing that were prayers in disguise, and the things people were saying to me that were, in fact, words from on high.

A poem by Rumi says, "There are hundreds of ways to kneel and kiss the ground," and I have never been more certain of this in my life.[11] I am living it now, at least in fits and spurts. I always wondered how the Bible could exhort us to pray without ceasing, and now I know. Prayer is not the words you say or how often you say them. Prayer is an attitude with which you move through life. It's a way of seeing your world. It's a willingness to let things into your heart, and it's the bravery to let things go. It's the clarity to see Jesus in the face of a stranger and humanity in the face of an enemy. It's the inexplicable hope that weasels its way into a wounded heart. It is a posture of surrender and a stance of audacious determination. It is any expression of gratitude. It is courage and belief, imagination and creativity. Prayer is any way by which we participate in God or engage God's redemptive activity or let ourselves give way to love.

I am telling you all of this because Jesus was once praying in a certain place, so says our text today—and I'm sure, by the way, that this "certain place" was just as crucial to his prayer as the actual words—and he was holding sacred space for himself and God when the disciples asked him how to pray. They wanted to be taught, and Jesus did the strangest thing. He didn't tell them a single thing about the mechanics: closed eyes versus open eyes, bowed heads versus raised faces, orderly lines versus speaking in tongues, raised arms versus clasped hands, silence versus naming and claiming, singing and smiling versus solemn whispers, community versus solitude. All Jesus did was a recite a simple little prayer, and then, go figure, tell a parable.

What were those words about, those words we routinely call the Lord's Prayer? Are they magic words, the abracadabra of prayer? Of course not. Do they represent some kind of formula—a list of the most important prayer elements: praise, supplication, confession, petition, what have you? No, I don't think formulas and lists are what this is about.

Think ahead to the parable, where Jesus is essentially saying, "Don't you know that your Father in heaven *knows how* to give good gifts to his children?" I think Jesus' point is this: Relax. Prayer is easy. All you've got to do is ask. It will be given. Seek. You will find. Knock. The door will open.

If it doesn't seem that easy for you, maybe you're trying too hard. Scale back. Return to the simplicity of a God who is interested in you, who would never hand out scorpions when you're asking for eggs. Ask for an egg, and he's more likely to give you a whole breakfast taco. That is God, and if God doesn't seem that way to you, drop all your other spiritual efforts and ideas until you find the God of grace and mercy again. Better yet, let Grace find you.

The Lord's Prayer, consequently, isn't something to dissect, analyze, or mimic. It's something to free-fall into with confidence and relief. It's something to recite when all your other words have failed you, or it's one of the ways to open your mouth with your face pointed to heaven, or it's a reminder that only a few words will do just fine, that this isn't rocket science or any kind of science; it is art. Prayer is art, and finger paints and Crayolas will land you a treasured spot on God's refrigerator door just as readily as water-color and oils. You don't have to push the right button to open the doorway between the worlds; the door is open. No incantations are necessary—just the words we say and repeat, say and repeat, to help wake us up to the God who has not once slumbered through any moment of our lives.

I know there's the whole business of unanswered prayers that sends us into a confused muddle about prayer, and I get that. I mean, boy, do I ever get that. I've had some nasty, curve-ball lack of answers thrown my way, and they've knocked me off-balance many a time. I've wanted to give up on praying, just to spare myself the disappointment. All I know for sure about that is I've *also* seen a few miracles and that something I cannot explain keeps drawing me back into the posture of prayer.

The Lord's Prayer isn't about how to say the perfect prayer; the Lord's Prayer is a reminder to us of prayer's simplicity. Jesus illustrates this with a few little stories: asking a friend for bread, approaching your father for an egg, knocking on a door and watching it swing open. See how this is easy, regular, ordinary stuff? Somehow we've made it so hard to ask for what we want and so complicated to see God, but Jesus encourages us to recover what the New International Version calls "shameless audacity," and he reassures us that God is good and the Holy Spirit is on its way.

Lately, "dear God" has been creeping its way back into my journal. Organically. Naturally. Fittingly. I realize I've missed those more direct prayers. And yet I am grateful, too, for their absence because I have learned how to pray in so many new ways.

Or, as Rumi would put it,

Today, like every other day, we wake up empty
and frightened. Don't open the door to the study
and begin reading. Take down a musical instrument.
Let the beauty we love be what we do.
There are hundreds of ways to kneel and kiss the ground.
The breeze at dawn has secrets to tell you.
Don't go back to sleep.
You must ask for what you really want.
Don't go back to sleep.
People are going back and forth across the doorsill

where the two worlds touch.
The door is round and open.
Don't go back to sleep.[12]

Amen.

5
spirit:
trust in preaching

It is challenging to write about trust because I don't know *how* to trust. (Do you?) Who wants to hear what the fish has to say about flying through the air, and who wants to hear what the fretter has to say about trust?

And yet I am not entirely unpracticed. Maybe you can relate to the seesaw ride of faith: up we go, and down we fall again and again almost involuntarily. I don't know if it has ever worked for you—*trying* to have more faith—but I can't recall it ever working for me. Gritting my teeth to produce trust backfires every time. *Trying* often leaves me wallowing in more doubt than when I first began, and—bonus!—gives me the added weight of guilt for having tried a thing and failed.

And yet trust is crucial to the act of preaching. Without it, your preaching's got no spirit, no wind, no oomph, nothing bigger than you at play, no guidance. Or, to say it more clearly, trust is crucial to the act of living, as preaching is only one small component of a life. Without trust, your life's got no spirit, no wind, no oomph, nothing bigger than you at play, no guidance.

So if trust is crucial but we cannot self-induce it, are we all screwed? Of course we can *ask* for it, which I recommend; however, I don't know if you've noticed this yet, but God rarely seems to be in the same *hurry* that we are. Ask for faith, yes, but don't expect it to arrive in the mail tomorrow.

I can honestly report that I am currently living with a much larger trust than I have lived with before, and while I don't know what to tell you about how to acquire faith, I can tell you what happened to me: I have spent most of a life paralyzed by self-doubt. I feared my impulses and my instincts, I doubted my opinions, I was suspicious of all my feelings, I second-guessed myself, I was too shy to speak up, and if I did speak, I said what I had to say like it was all an apology. I made so certain never to step on anybody's toes that you could barely call my movement *walking*. It was more like a dodging shuffle, getting out of everyone else's way with little understanding of my own way.

The church reinforced this self-doubt shuffle by continually reminding me that I was a sinner (i.e., someone *not* to be trusted) and that my heart was "deceitful above all things and desperately wicked." Therefore, recovering from the crippling effects of self-suspicion was a long and arduous journey. For starters, reclaiming my trustworthiness felt arrogant. It also seemed selfish, self-absorbed, and narcissistic. Additionally, as I became increasingly adamant that I wanted only authentic encounters with the divine, not the manufactured encounters that I seemed to be expected to have, I feared that my insistence on genuine God-encounters would disappoint or lead me away from faith altogether. I was terrified that following my heart would lead me astray.

What I discovered instead is that trusting myself was the first step to a more authentic trust of God. So much of religion teaches us to deny our experiences, to sacrifice our instincts in service of dogma, but I have found this to be the exact backwards approach to coming to know the bigness of God. Religion has taught us our smallness versus God's bigness, but our human instinct is to grow, and our spiritual drive is to expand, soar, enlarge, swell.

My friend Jenny once looked me in the eye and said, "You are so trustworthy," and with that statement she tipped my self-perception in a brand-new direction. My inner reaction to her declaration was an incredulous, "I am?" but eventually I could whisper to myself, "I am." I am trustworthy. I can be trusted. That doesn't mean I always get it right. It does mean that I choose to tell the truth as best I can, that I admit to myself and to others when I get it wrong, and that I live with an open heart.

In my youth I was profoundly influenced by a speaker who emphasized God as I AM WHO I AM (from Exodus 3:14), and the speaker concluded that the I AM of God led to the I AM NOT of humanity. It was self-negation in service of worship, and as an angst-ridden youth looking for something bigger and better to belong to than my awkward and insecure adolescence, this sounded good, right, and comforting: God is. I am not. And while that perspective may have served a purpose for a while, I now see such self put-down as counter to the spiritually awake life. The "I AM" of God leads to the "I am" of me and, more important, the "I am" of humanity.

I am (we are) created in God's image.

I am beloved.

I am unique.

I am child of God.

I am who I am because God is who God, is and both of these are beautiful.

This is not self-worship. To show reverence for creation is to appreciate and honor the Creator (whether you have a name for God or not). Richard Rohr comments that in our society,

> We're tremendously underconfident about what it means to be human . . . . When civilization has flourished, when great music, art, and literature have emerged, it's always when human beings have felt good about being human. Human is something great to be. Being human is just a little less than God (Psalm 8:5). That's exactly what faith gives us, a kind of extraordinary dignity. It gives us a sense of our own meaning: religion calls us "sons and daughters of God."[13]

This is how I have come to see it: I do not serve you or humanity or God by reducing my shimmer. The world only shines brighter when we all shine.

I do not mean to suggest that I never sin or make mistakes. I do mean to suggest that the image of God implanted in my soul by the creator is *way bigger* than my foibles. I do mean to suggest that the goodness of God within me is light and joy, and I would do well to heed it. I do mean to suggest that the divine spark I possess as the beloved of God is beautiful and trustworthy. It is alive and well, and I sure need to stop bottling that shimmer up for fear that she won't get it all quite right. I do mean to suggest that I have God-power in me, and so do you, and it is high time we stop giving our power away with this obsessive fretting about sin.

News flash: Authentic religious repentance is not what happens when you make yourself feel bad about yourself. Repentance is what happens when something Holy taps you unexpectedly on the shoulder and tells you, "Um, turn around and go this way now. That old path isn't working for you," and when the new way opens it is relief, it is light beam, it is mercy.

In other words, there is no fear when you are walking the God-path of love, which is how 1 John puts it. You don't have to be afraid of yourself. You don't have to punish your doubt or keep your feelings about God caged in a cell. You can bring all that you are and all that you have experienced and all that you think to the table with God. In fact, you must do that. As long as you leave yourself behind to submit blindly to what you are told about God, that isn't relationship. Relationship happens when two whole people engage one another.

To trust yourself, to be yourself, to become yourself is neither narcissistic nor prideful. It is mature faith. It is discovering who you were meant to be as the fullest expression of honoring the One who created you.

I find that the more I trust myself, my voice, my passion, the still small voice that whispers within me, the more Grace absolutely takes me by surprise. I literally feel that I am being carried through this life as if by a Wind. On my doubtful days, I call the experience of being carried Serendipity, Beauty, or Joy. On my faith-filled days, I call it God. Either way, my trust grows ever larger.

The Faith You Have

Luke 17:5-6 (Covenant Baptist Church)

Do you know how big a mustard seed is? Well, it is teeny tiny, no bigger than a speck. We might be inclined to believe that Jesus is ridiculing, scolding, or, at the very least, challenging the disciples' faith or their lack thereof, as if he were saying, "Look, if you could muster up even a mustard seed's worth, you could do miracles, you trust-limp wimps! Where are your faith muscles? I don't even want to waste my time on the likes of you!"

We might hear that in Jesus' tone except, of course, we happen to know that these are the men on whom Jesus did waste time. Again and again, he spent time with these fellows whether they were full of faith or all dried out.

The disciples, as far as I can tell, were not really one or the other. Sometimes they had enough faith to drop their fishing nets, leave their former lives behind, and follow a man they hardly knew. Other times you could catch them rolling their eyes when Jesus finished a story, because yet again they had missed the point.

Sometimes a disciple was someone who could walk on water, and sometimes a disciple was someone who straight sank until the goodness of the Lord grabbed him by the wrists and kept him from drowning. Sometimes a disciple was someone who gave up everything to serve the Lord, and sometimes a disciple was someone who got his stomach worked into an anxious knot when one jar of alabaster was wasted on the good Lord's unshowered head. Sometimes a disciple was one who risked his neck to stay faithful, and sometimes a disciple was someone who fled from the scene as soon as soldiers showed up to take God away. Sometimes a disciple was someone who spoke truth boldly, and sometimes a disciple was someone who got cold feet and a dry mouth in front of one small servant girl in a courtyard right when Jesus could have used his support the most.

I reckon this roller coaster ride of faith was making the disciples a bit sick of their own selves, and that is what prompted them with queasy stomachs to approach the Lord and ask/beg, "Increase our faith! Please!" They were tired of being so up, then down, so right, then wrong, so brave, then squeamish, so sure, then wary. They were frustrated, not to mention nauseated. They were hoping for something easier on the intestines, something that didn't make them feel as if they were being dragged willy-nilly this way and that by the faith they were hanging on to by a thread.

"Increase our faith!" the disciples demanded because they did not want to give up, but neither did they want to keep running, then tripping, standing, then falling. If only they had *more faith*, surely life would settle down along with their blood pressure, and finally they'd be disciples for real.

So far, they spent half their time mesmerized by their master and the other half knowing they must seem like a joke to the world because of their inability to master the doubt and fear and lack of understanding that still plagued their steps. And so they asked Jesus, "Please fix this. We are broken, see?"

Only Jesus does no such fixing. (Or does he?) He says to them, each and every one, "All you need is a mustard seed of faith. A teeny, tiny mustard seed amount will do." For Jesus knew that, as many times as these disciples had sunk, there were other occasions on which they had soared, so when they asked for more, he told them, "You've already got enough." Even the most doubt-ravaged among us have got at least a kernel or a poppy seed or a molecule of faith, and any faith at all can lead to wonders. This is the good news.

The bad news is that disciples today look pretty much the same as disciples then, and asking Jesus for faith never did level out the roller coaster. Our faith still goes up and down, up and down.

Every time a disciple goes plummeting down, she reaches her hand into her pocket to see if, at the very least, the seed's still there. It is.

The seed is there because you didn't plant it. God did. The seed of faith was a gift to you, and even in your darkest, most doubt-plagued hours, there are tiny, invisible roots that keep your seed buried deep within the soil of your becoming. It's not your responsibility to hold on to it. It holds on to you, even when you think it is lost for good. The seed is there, and a seed is all you need.

Of course, all this begs the question, then why the heck aren't there more mulberry trees whizzing across the room and out towards the sea, like a scene from Professor Flitwick's classroom in Harry Potter? If we've got the magic seed, where is the magic?

I have exactly five hunches about that.

1. God's magic doesn't always match our ideas about what needs to happen. Keep fingering that little seed tucked in your pocket, and on rare occasions this will actually make sense to you, though probably not for long.

2. We forget to even ask. Seriously, I think we don't know the Power inside us, and so we don't even bother to look up at our world and ask the question, "What is it around here that needs to be uprooted? I think I'll place my hand on that and pray."

3. The magic is coming. We don't always see it clearly right now, but Healing is on its way. The answers will show themselves when you've been made ready to hear them. The light is coming. Just after the dark of night, you can count on the sunrise.

4. The magic is already here. Yep, we are surrounded by goodness and miracle, but we forget to pay attention. The more often you touch that seed of faith, the more you'll be able to see what is already happening.

5. The rest is mystery, and if it were any clearer, it wouldn't be called faith—this slippery, elusive thing that carries us through the shadows and holds on to us no matter how often we lose our grip.

The point is not so much the words Jesus and his disciples exchanged but that they exchanged them. The disciples brought the smallness of their faith to him, he met their smallness with a largeness of heart, and this union made things fly.

We've developed a quirky sense of religious competition that makes us hide our small faith rather than expose it, flaunt confidence rather than confess our fear, puff out our chest rather than say what we need. But when we begin honestly, reach into our pockets, take out our seeds, and show them to one another, saying, "Look. This is all I have," that is when things begin to happen.

I don't know about you, but I'm often able to believe for my friends what I cannot believe for myself. I can *see* that they've got the seed of faith and that the seed is enough, even when they can't see it. It is in letting the smallness of my faith meet the smallness of your faith that we begin to learn we *are* people of faith, despite the fears that constantly shrink us. We bring the smallness of what we've got right before Jesus' nose, and instead of shaming us, he smiles and says, "That'll do, child; that'll do."

Amen.

As-You-Go Healing

Luke 17:11-19 (Covenant Baptist Church)

"As they went, they were made clean," so the story goes. Here is the thing about as-you-go healing: First of all, it is how most of us are healed. Not in the blink of an eye in a split-second encounter with God, but on the journey, along the way, going towards wherever it is God has instructed us to go. We are healed along the path of fidelity, or what Eugene Peterson calls "a long obedience in the same direction."[14] It is in the going, as we plod along, that we heal. Even if we are a bit cynical or skeptical or reluctant as we put one foot in front of the other, we will often be surprised at what happens along the way.

Sometimes, or often, this as-you-go healing is so gradual that we hardly recognize it is happening until we look down one day at our once-crusted skin and see that it is fresh and clean, and we don't even know when it happened, the alteration from disease to glory. Like a piercing headache, you curse the pain when it is there, wanting it to leave you, but once the pounding begins to fade, you don't always notice it is happening until suddenly it occurs to you, "I'm not in pain anymore."

This is what I imagine happened to these fellows in Luke 17. They were lepers for years and years, and then they took one long walk that gradually, imperceptibly cleaned them out until they looked down and were startled by the new look of their own hands and legs.

I wonder how long they stayed there, stopped in their tracks, marveling, running giddy fingertips over baby-fresh skin. After smelling of rotting flesh for far too long, did they now smell like infants? But I also wonder how disappointed they were earlier in the day, having worked up the courage to call out to Jesus, and then seemingly being turned away and told to go see the priest instead.

Another thing about as-you-go healing is that sometimes you forget to say thank you. You may feel the inner relief when you notice what has happened to you, but you may never express it out loud. You may even feel bitter that it took so blasted long.

But for those who do come back, who turn, praise, fall to their knees, and say the words, "Thank you, thank you, thanks be to my God"—for those who do *that*, then things start to get interesting.

When you return to say thanks, you learn that there is more to heal. Notice how Jesus tells the already-healed leper, "Get up and go on your way; your faith has made you well," as if *something else* happened other than the healing we already know about, the one we could see with our eyes. Was this man healed on the inside too? Did the power of God course through his veins a second time, rearrange his inner life in ways we'll never know, in ways perhaps the man himself didn't even know to ask for? That is what I think is happening right here: a second, further healing.

And notice how similar Jesus' instructions sound compared to the first time: "Go on your way." Once again, the command to go. Keep walking, keep traversing, and who knows what else might heal along the way? A third, a fourth, a fifth miracle may meet you on the road.

As best I can tell, the healing we need from Jesus is always onion-layers deep because the pain and trauma and evil we have endured is layers deep too, and in nearly every human case I know, healing happens bit by bit, layer by layer, as you go, and *as you give thanks*.

Did you notice how Jesus links gratitude and faith in this event? The man returns to say thank you, and Jesus calls this faith. "Your faith has made you well," he says. Sometimes we think of faith as a daunting, difficult thing reserved for the doubtless; we could never attain it. But what if faith *is* gratitude? What if expanding our capacity for gratitude is an expansion of our faith?

The world can be a cruel place, and I would never act as if gratitude is always easy. I would never be flippant about evil, pain, or suffering, never naïve about the complexities of injustice, mental illness, strained relationships, chronic illness, etc. as if one can just *feel* grateful amid the fatigue of distress.

We have no idea how that leper *felt*. For all we know, he was confused that Jesus sent him away or embarrassed that he was Samaritan or ashamed of his past. All we really know for sure is that he took his transfigured body back to the feet of Jesus and made himself open his mouth and say with his words what he was thankful for.

Gratitude changes things. It is not just a nifty trick for avoiding the reality of pain. It is a real tool for transforming perspective, unlocking further healing, and significantly increasing your joy.

I only have the guts to suggest this to you because I've literally tried it in my darkest hours and seen what it can do, the faith of being thankful. I'm not saying I got any instant fixes from stopping to say thanks. But I do think we can get a bit of tunnel vision when we are going through something hard, and all we see is the negative with no sign of light at the end. Or sometimes we get the same tunnel vision just going through the mundane. Gratitude is something we have to wake up to; we're rarely already wired to be alert to the good. We have to practice activating that kind of electricity, but once we flip the switch, such a simple act can unleash power.

This does not mean grateful people always feel good. We still have bad days, want-to-stay-in-bed days, despair-of-consistent-happiness days. We all have hours or seasons where we crumple. But the lonesome hour does not define us, because by practicing gratitude, we escape the illusion that our lives are the sum total of our failures, disappointments, and the grievances against us. We are *more* than all the sorrows and evil we have borne, and as we say thank you for the kindnesses we have known, those long-lived sorrows resurface in such a way that they might begin to be healed over time.

Though it may sound easier to attain gratitude than to have the faith to heal, gratitude requires intentionality, the energy to repent and to turn around from your self-focused walking and express to another, "I am grateful for the way you intersected my journey." Maybe the other nine healed lepers were grateful, at least as a fleeting thought, but they did not recognize that expressing it out loud would lodge the thankfulness and joy past the surface into a deeper place. And while they got their first miracle, they may have sealed themselves off from further joy by their failure to fully appreciate what they had been given.

When we get stuck in a mucky place, there are ways we can begin to wedge ourselves forward into the healing light of God. Instead of making a mental list of what we still need, we can make lists of what we have. Instead of drawing a map of where we need to go, we can map how far we have come. Instead of complaining, we can make a phone call or write a note to someone who has done something we appreciate. Instead of despairing over how our lives are going, we can pay attention to someone else's life long enough to say, "I am thankful for you." Instead of scurrying ahead with a scowl, we can pause and smile. This is no quick fix or easy solution; as-you-go healing may be for you a far longer road than you ever wanted it to be. But you can, by small acts of gratitude, keep positioning yourself in a place to receive some cleansing.

Our text adds this footnote: "And he was a Samaritan." I take that to mean, in part, that it matters not who you are or where you come from or how unlikely your healing is. Anyone can experience healing, and anyone can choose to rejoice. Perhaps because he had come from such a lowly place, gratitude was more readily this man's response.

Whoever you are, wherever you've come from, however unlikely your healing, I suspect there is at least one thing—tiny as it may be—worth thanking God for or, if you're mad at God, one thing worth expressing gratitude for, even if you don't address the thanks to anyone specific. Whoever you are, wherever you've come from, however unlikely your healing, I pray this prayer for you today: that as you go along your way, you may heal. That however hard the journey, there may be moments where you can smile, and that with each smile, you would be watering the seed of faith, even if you don't realize that is what your smiles are capable of. I pray that, as you walk along, Jesus or Miracle or Love would meet you on the road, not once, not twice, but again and again and again, and that layer by layer by deep-buried layer, you would be made well. Amen.

BRAIN:
imagination in preaching

We generally think preachers should be smart, educated, well read, biblically literate, and theologically sound. I'd offer a resounding *yes* to all of the above, but I would also add that these otherwise good qualities are liable to shut our imagination down if we let them dominate our preaching or our living, and that would be a tragic misuse of our knowledge. No one will care that you have mastered Greek if you have lost your sense of wonder. Extensive vocabulary be damned if you lack the capacity to create anything beautiful with it. This is what we must recapture if we are to preach rather than drone: how to sit like wide-eyed children before Scripture, glowing with discovery and curiosity. If you're just a scholar who squints your eyes in critique, you've shut out half your vision.

Imagination is key. Imagination is like a magnifying glass, or a set of 3D lenses, or a way to close your eyes and dream. It is what allows us to hold Scripture as if it were a prism, and suddenly we see shades of color where before we only saw empty space. Imagination is the portal by which we enter the story and the story enters us. Imagination unlocks the door between dead letters and living words.

We do not invite imagination into preaching merely to ensure an engaging sermon. We invite imagination because we are teaching people *how* to read their Bibles. We are saying, "Lighten up! Relax! Have fun! Engage! A little irreverence won't call down any lightning." We are showing people how to be unafraid of the sacred text, how to digest it, how to love it, how to live it, how to retell it as their own.

This is what we do with Scripture as the people of God: We allow it to awaken us. We enter it as characters ourselves. We ask it questions. We make guesses—sometimes wild guesses—at its meaning. We bring our hopes and fears and ideas into the reading with us. When done blindly, this can be detrimental eisegesis—reading our own preconceptions and prejudices into the Bible—but when done passionately and prayerfully and patiently, it is a magical dance by which the inspired Word inspires us.

Dull preaching, no matter how smart, is still dull. We don't want that, my friends. We want the Holy Spirit. We want power. We want a living, breathing Scripture to poke out an appearance from the pulpit, every time if possible. Thus we invite creativity like pebbles to fall into the pools of our consciousness and to ripple out into what we write and say and embody about the faith. When we engage creatively in interpretation, we become co-creators with God. Like Adam naming the animals, we look at what God has given us, then give these experiences names of our own that arise from within us. God, I believe, invites this high level of participation. We do not merely receive the Scriptures as passive listeners; we mix ourselves in with the words so that the powerful "Let there be" of God's voice might create us anew every time we read.

Producing a sermon is hard work, and there are all kinds of schemata and schedules one can follow to aid the weekly sermon-writing process. These disciplines can help a little, but they don't matter nearly as much as coming to learn and understand and bolster your own creative process. Creativity is generally a bit messy and not too obedient to the calendar. Learn to trust yourself. When I was driving down the road the week before All Saints' Day, and something inside told me, "Pull over into this cemetery and write about All Saints' Day there," I obeyed the voice and sat among the tombstones, reflecting on death and remembrance and sainthood. This was not an event or setting I had planned, but it was important. Trust where you are being led and what you are drawn to say. Every act of trust invites more mystery, more power, more imagination.

Sprinkling your own imagination into the story can feel a little sacrilegious at first, but keep at it. Eventually you will *feel* the invitation, the pull of Scripture to enter the text like an eager child on the playground. Eventually you will start to have fun.

You may not feel like a very creative person, but you are, in fact, quite creative. I am certain of this. It was how you were created, to be a mini-creator in the image and likeness of the One who created you. You may be out of touch with your creativity, because adulthood tends to undervalue imagination and overvalue efficiency, but the good news is that all of us were once children, and we can find our way back to the heart of a child if we try. Recover the part of you that used to play pretend and build forts and invent games and believe in ghosts. If it is a long recovery process, so be it. I tend to think that when Jesus welcomed the little children and said the kingdom of heaven belonged to them, it was a gentle intervention for the rest of us so that we might come to recognize ourselves as recovering adults. Some of us are so bad off that we need a twelve-step program just to take a break from thinking we must run the world. Children do not try to keep things running; they are much too sobered up to the wonder of reality to hallucinate about things like power and control. Children bury their toes in sandboxes just to feel the strange pleasure of cool grit on their skin. Children hop over cracks in the sidewalk just to make the journey home more exciting. Children laugh out loud just because they want to and say what they think because it has never occurred to them to say anything else. It is the child's brain and Adam's first-day eyes that we want to bring to the text when we explore it.

Take your Bible out to the swing set of your mind, give it a push, and let it fly. Don't be so afraid of heights. You won't fall on your face if you get playful, and even if you do, you're young enough at heart to get back up and play some more.

Sometimes, when I feel stuck on a particular sermon, I set aside my notes and I get out a blank sheet of white paper. Then I open a box of crayons, and, with the Scripture fresh on my mind, I begin to color whatever comes to me. I listen to which colors draw me—there is no rhyme or reason to what I create. I simply go with my gut. I do this to unlock the part of my brain I was undoubtedly ignoring in my stuckness.

There are other ways I unstick my stuckness—writing a poem about the text, taking a walk, working outside, inventing a short story on the spot, putting aside the laptop and picking up a pencil. Anything that invites playfulness, freedom, or creativity back into the sermon-writing process can help.

Of course, this will not work for you at all if you aren't simultaneously practicing an imaginative approach to *life*. If you live stuck inside four white concrete walls without windows, if you never sink your fingers into Play-Doh, never ask "why" incessantly, never dance a little when you're alone, then, chances are, your creative juices are dammed up in some nearly unreachable place. Imagination is generally the thing that unsticks us during life's dilemmas. It's the random burst of insight that gives us permission to do life as no one has ever done it before. It's the energy that lets us think outside the box, fight evil in new ways, find life in unexpected places, and stop repeating the same old patterns that were getting us nowhere.

An example of this is when I got stuck in some anger, and I couldn't figure out how to express it or get myself past it. It felt like a big swirling black mass that I couldn't touch or expunge. For me, ignoring the anger was "easy," but in the end I knew I hadn't actually moved it anywhere. It was simmering within, slowly spreading poison. So I asked friends for input: what did they do when they were feeling angry and needing to get it out somehow? One person said that when her friend was going through something dark, she wanted to break plates. So they did it together. They got a stack of plates and smashed them on the back porch. Another friend told me that in her family they get a box of Teddy Grahams, and then they eat off the heads and limbs of the bear crackers with vicious intention. Or they pick up pillows and whack things. Someone I know goes out to a secluded place and screams at God. I came up with a few ideas of my own and tried them all: I went to the batting cages and hit balls with vengeance. I climbed into the shower, and with the sound of the vent and the running water to muffle things, I felt that I had the permission to scream at last. I walked in the woods where no one was around, and I hurled rocks into the trees and said to my hurts, "Take that!" I bought markers that were made for writing on mirrors, and I wrote on a mirror the things that I could never work up the nerve to put on a journal page, and then I immediately wiped it clean. I wrote on the mirror, wiped it away, wrote, wiped, wrote, wiped. The fact that the words didn't have any permanence to them set me free, and the process was cathartic. I also wrote words on paper. I would read the words again and again until I felt that I was finished hearing them, and then I would tear the paper into shreds and throw it to the wind. I got out dark colors and scribbled all over the page, the way a two-year-old scribbles, only I was pressing harder and I knew that I was expressing what I had no words to say.

I don't know if this will surprise you, but I am predominately a left-brained thinker. I like logic, logarithms, straight lines, and the linear. In high school, I was an algebra master. Math and I got along quite well. I love its reliability, its cleanliness, its stark precision; it loves me for my attention to detail, my focused diligence, and my capacity for rule-following when I set my mind to it. Unfortunately, algebra only works well when there is a set answer to x = _____ and when the right methods will get you to the right answer every time. So far, life is turning out to be far more complicated than my algebra textbook, and hence I am now on a lifelong journey of accepting the complex science of an artful life.

Creativity is the part of us that says, "I refuse to stay stuck, be bored, or regurgitate clichés. I will enter the world and be alive in it, and I do not care if what I do is weird to the rest. This is me, being alive. This is me, fighting to hold on to life. This is me, being a unique creation of God's own design. This is me, saying to God, 'Why yes, I would love to name the animals. Thank you for asking.'"

Until the Morning Star Rises

2 Peter 1:16-19 (Transfiguration Sunday,
Covenant Baptist Church)

Today is Transfiguration Sunday, the Sunday before Ash Wednesday, the Sunday before Lent begins. To give you a refresher, the Transfiguration is when Jesus invites Peter, James, and John to join him atop a mountain to pray, and while there, he transfigures and begins to glow white. He is suddenly joined by Elijah and Moses, and the three of them begin chatting. (For a moment, seeing Moses, you might be reminded of the way Moses glowed too, coming down the mountain after meeting with God, so brilliant with light he had to wear a veil to shield the people.) Peter hastily suggests that he wants to build each one of them a tent, or a shelter. In none of the Gospel accounts does Jesus find this worthy of reply, so I imagine Jesus giving him the "Oh Peter" look, a facial expression, let's just say, that the disciples were accustomed to. Then the voice of God speaks, saying, "This is my Son, the Beloved, with him I am well-pleased. Listen to him." And as quickly as that, it's all over. Moses and Elijah are gone, and Jesus tells the disciples to keep this strange event under wraps until after the resurrection.

This odd little story about Jesus glimmering on a mountaintop pitches us forward onto the dusty, unglamorous road to Golgotha. And this hilltop incident is just mysterious and confusing enough that we might prefer to go ahead and keep it under wraps, even as a post-resurrection people, but Scripture encourages us otherwise. In the text we read this morning from 2 Peter, we are specifically told that we would do well to pay attention to this particular story, for it confirms the prophetic message. Second Peter 1:19 says, "You will do well to be attentive to this as to a lamp shining in a dark place, until the day dawns and the morning star rises in your hearts." The writer does little to make the story easier to understand, but for me, he makes it more enticing to try, because he calls this story a lamp shining in a dark place, and he attaches a promise to it about the day dawning and the morning star rising. And so with this promise of light dangling over the Transfiguration, I climb to the top of the mountain yet again, trailing Peter, James, and John. I rub the sleep out of my eyes and watch it all unfold with awakened wonder. (Care to join me?)

As I listen, the phrase, "Until the morning star rises in your hearts," tumbles around inside me like tennis balls in the dryer, rattling me loose, clanking in the ear of my heart, fluffing up an old flattened story for renewed wear.

I want to share with you the poem I wrote after listening to this text, a poem I call "Until the Morning Star Rises":

Keep watching the light
Until you become light.
Keep attending to the beaming of his face
Until you yourself are transfigured.
Keep positioning yourself
in line with the glow
until you feel a gleam
break forth in you.

Don't you ever build a tent
you silly rash Peters
chomping to do something
significant, anxious to bottle
up this extraordinary moment
for safe-keeping.

Give your miracles away
for free distribute the mercies
you have known.
Don't plop down inside
your big cozy tent
alone and safe,
your treasure secure.
No. No. No.
Run down that hill

like a wildfire, hot
while the power lasts,
spread burning love
lick the world
like flames, do not
veil yourself
like Moses even
when people ask you
to cover up—
such polite modesty
does not suit you
when your face is shining
with the afterglow
of God.

Glow, child, glow.
God is pleased with you.

At the bottom of the hill
your light will smack
hard into pain—people's
hurts, your own wounds
like a wall—they call it
the valley of the shadow
and it is dark there.
Run there anyway.
Don't speak too hastily
of Jesus or all you saw
up on the mountain.
It won't make much sense
if told in haste. Also:
no one will believe you.

So take your time meandering
among the masses, meeting
as many eyes as you can,
let your gaze be a window
into what you have seen.
Look back into their stare,
see more there
than you have ever seen before.
With those you meet exchange

small glimmers, tiny faith flickers.
Swap burdens. Share darkness.
Meld together.
Hold hands.
Journey on.

At some point in your wandering
you will begin to wonder
where all of this is going.
You will raise your face and
up ahead you will see
a rough, wood-carved cross:
this will shock you.
More even than the
darkness of the valley and
the friendship you found there,
this will shock you.

Jesus is hoisting
himself up onto it,
willingly, and he
is mouthing the words,
"Follow me,"
and you will protest,
"But, but the mountain!
You were glowing!
Let's go back.
Why didn't I tabernacle you
when I had the chance,
grab hold, keep you
encased with fabric
and poles, stake you
to the ground—make you stay?
Instead I lived loose
traveled light
made friends
and now you are
leaving us
with the sun setting
behind you,
possibly forever."

Silence.

Black Grief.

No reply.

You will close your eyes and
so will God in heaven,
sorrow overtaking sight,

but you will *hear* the earth
shake and rocks moan
and a great big veil
in the temple
will begin to rip.
You will hear it tearing
and it will be
to your ears like the
sound of pain and the
wailing of separation.

But it is not that.

It is the sound Moses heard
when he would rip
off his veil in the
presence of God, it is
the sound of sunshine
cracking over the surface of
the earth, it is the
sound of walls between heaven
and earth, walls between brothers
falling down at last,
it is the sound of
light beams shattering
blindness, it is the sound
of God dying, then rising
like a star in your heart.

Amen.

Wildflowers

Galatians 3:23-29 (Covenant Baptist Church)

There was once a girl who daily wandered the fields for her love of wildflowers. She would walk through the tall grasses that brushed her legs in the breeze, and she would try to quiet the noise in her head so that there was space enough inside her heart to absorb the fragrance and the color. She would take deep breaths and gaze, gaze, gaze as if to inhale the sights of the earth.

As she walked she would talk to the Artist who gave birth to this beauty. "Artist," she would say, "these Indian blankets are my favorite."

"Yes, I am fond of them too, and I can see how much you love them," the Artist would reply in a whisper that could only be felt, not heard.

"Did you make them just for me?" The girl would smile, feeling filled to the top with love and happiness.

"Yes," answered the Artist, "and no. I made them for you because I knew they would touch your heart. But I also made them for me, and I made them just because, and I made them for all the boys and girls who delight in the color red, and I made them for the lonely person in need of brightness, and I made them for the distracted driver on the highway, and I made them for no reason at all, and then I made them just especially for you, my sweet, and all these things are true."

"Mmm." The girl simply nodded her head, for she was wise beyond her years and knew this mystery might reveal itself in time if only she believed.

"Is it wrong to have a favorite?" she asked most sincerely, for she was a sensitive girl and was worried that the orange, white, pink, and blue flowers might feel neglected due to her devotion to the Indian blanket.

"No, no, my child. Your heart is drawn to those particular flowers for a reason, and you should always listen to your heart. Every wildflower needs a steady and faithful admirer. I send others to tend to the bluebonnets, some to the sunflowers, still others to the foxgloves. Do not neglect your duty to love what you desire to love."

The girl chewed her lip thoughtfully, and she gingerly fingered a particularly vibrant yellow flower. "I do love them all, you know," she offered upon further reflection.

"As do I. As do I," answered the Artist. "There is room in my heart for every variety to be a distinct favorite."

The girl pondered this, and though slightly confused by it all, she felt as though her heart were stretching. "And what about the flowers that grow in hidden places that no one ever sees? Why did you make those?" she asked the Artist.

"For pleasure, for the chance of discovery, for the fun of hidden beauty, because those very spots were begging for color, because *I* can see those places, and for five hundred more reasons."

At that moment, a bird soared in a circle over her head, and up she looked, watching it float upon its wings. She kept walking, but she was no longer looking down, and that is how it came to pass that she tumbled right into a cactus clump before she could stop herself. "Ahh!" she cried and said some words that pleasant girls do not often say, but as it was only her, the flowers, and the Artist, she did not bother to apologize. The Artist quite nearly chuckled, but managed to hold it in and whispered a sympathetic sigh instead, only she did not hear him at all for she was too busy staring in dismay at her now-barbed legs.

How could there possibly be that many needles in one small plant? she wondered to herself along with every other person who has ever tangled with a cactus. It really didn't seem possible, but there they were, seemingly countless spines stuck in her skin, and she set about the tedious task of plucking the painful stickers out one by one by one. "What I really want to know," she muttered rather irritably under her breath, her prior serenity less intact, "is why the dickens did you ever make cacti?"

Annoyingly, the Artist was smiling. "That is for me to know and you to ponder for many years."

The girl rolled her eyes. The Artist waited patiently. She stormed off in a huff, and it was many, many years before she returned to the fields where the wildflowers bloomed in spring. She had grown older and taller. The Artist had not changed at all, and there he was, waiting for her still. She nearly did not recognize him, it had been so long, but he knew her at once, and the breezes stirred in joy at her arrival. "Hello," he whispered, but she had forgotten how to listen, and at first she did not hear him.

She was distracted with the busy mind and the heavy burdens so many people come to carry once they become older. She ran her fingers listlessly through the tall grasses, not even noticing them, until a red and yellow circle of petals stopped her in her tracks: an Indian blanket, and suddenly the wind and the sunshine and the dirt of the earth were all speaking to her, and she could hear them. She inhaled the fragrance, the feel, and the fellowship of living things. "Artist!" she breathed, not to summon him, for he was already there, but because she recognized him.

He laughed with delight, and, relieved to see that he wasn't angry at her long absence, she suddenly wanted to tell him everything, all the reasons she left, all the reasons she hadn't come back, everything that had happened between the times, but the words caught in her throat, and to her relief, she could tell: he already knew, without it being said.

And so they walked the fields in silence, until they came upon a large bunch of cacti, where the girl stopped. It was just the right time, and the large yellow and orange cactus blooms were just now exploding into the open. But she was gazing past the petals to the clusters of spines. "I have met a number of cacti in real life," she told the Artist gravely.

"Yes," the Artist said, nodding.

"People who prick and hurt and wound and stick. Also, people who are unsightly. People who seem out of place among flowers. People who get in the way and block the path. People who intrude on your serenity."

"Yes," the Artist said, nodding.

"I'm still pondering why you put them here."

"Yes." The Artist nodded again.

"And yet you feed and water and shine upon them too, just like all the other life."

"Yes, I do. Of course I do," said the Artist.

"Today I see even the cacti are blooming."

"Yes, I wondered if you would notice that." The Artist smiled.

"And sometimes I think you're especially *fond*, even of the cactus?"

"Yes. Yes I am."

"I still do not quite understand." She wrinkled her nose.

"That is for me to know and you to ponder."

"I understand more than I used to," she added hopefully.

"Yes, yes you do," and at that the Artist went silent for a very long time and the girl admired the blooms between the spines, all the while careful not to step too close.

In Christ Jesus you are all children of God through faith. As many of you as were baptized into Christ have clothed yourselves with Christ. There is no longer Jew or Greek, there is no longer slave or free, there is no longer male and female; for all of you are one in Christ Jesus. And if you belong to Christ, then you are Abraham's offspring, heirs according to the promise. (Gal 3:26-29)

May the wildflower variety of people in this world fill your heart with wonder. May you see all the color and fragrances and diversity for the beautiful thing that it is; may you recognize the one Artist whose glory each bloom reflects. May you never wish for all one kind of flower to the extinction of the others. May you never shun an unsightly plant. When you see a thing you do not understand, open your heart wider, then wider. Trust that someday, these mysteries will become known.

May you embrace the world as your God has embraced you. May you see the fingerprints of the Artist everywhere you look, for the fingerprints are there, in every corner. May you acquire reverence for all living things, even and most especially those people who intrude on your serenity. To God be the glory, Amen.

7

Bones:
memory in preaching

Bones Last a Long time. When you say you know or believe something down in your bones, you mean you really know it, and you can recall or remember it again even when you seem to have forgotten. It means it has sunk down deep, that if you were stripped to your skeleton, it would still be there. This kind of knowing is etched into your ribcage, tattooed with the ink of your marrow onto your being so that it will outlast your last breath. If your body were burnt up in flames, this is what your ash would be made of.

The best preaching taps deeps into the marrow of our memories. When we receive a stroke of insight and think we are saying something new, really we are saying something very, very old. We are forever recycling the wisdom of our foremothers and forefathers. We are always speaking out of what we already knew deep inside. We are continually drawing from a well that existed long before we did and will continue to exist long after we are gone.

This is why doing traditional research for a sermon rarely produces my best work—it is too surface level, too right now, too narrowly focused on the topic at hand. My strongest sermon material comes from what I am planting into my being *as I walk through life*—the books I read purely for the way they ignite my soul, the observations I make about humanity and nature *just because* I am interested, the lessons I learn while slogging through my own foibles. These are the things I gather like seed and then wait to see what sprouts. When I do this, I feel that I am accessing a flow of energy bigger than myself and bigger than one sermon; I am brushing shoulders with ancient wisdom and giving it chance to be rebirthed in me. I am tapping our collective memory and hoping to recall it to our consciousness.

God dwells in the collective memory—a presence we *know* in a deep, indescribable way—and the preacher serves our knowing by helping us recollect the fragments of divinity that run through our inner streams.

This is also why I rely on image rather than illustration in my preaching. Illustrations are generally stories or bits of information that illuminate an idea—they emphasize, persuade, or explain a point, assisting the smooth transfer of thought from preacher to listener.

I prefer image because I am not trying to transfer my ideas to someone else when I preach. Most of the time, my sermon's "point," if it has a clear one, is an idea my congregation *already* agrees with. It is something they know, and I am wasting breath to try to convince them of the validity of my thought. What I want to do instead is carve out a space in the midst of chaotic living where we can encounter the holy.

Preachers often expend a lot of energy looking for incredible stories or fascinating facts to bolster their sermons, but I do not believe people come to the hour of worship to learn something new. If they wanted cute stories or trivia, they could find them on the Internet. I think they come to worship looking for God. They (we) are tired of God seeming so elusive. They (we) are often frustrated that it can be so damn hard to hold on to faith.

Preaching hopes to help people taste God, smell God, feel God, see God, hear God. This is the power of an image; it evokes what we *know* that we might experience more fully what we do not yet know down in our bones. People do not yet know (for certain) that God is reliable, but without even trying, they trust the sunrise. Remind them that God is sunrise. People do not think they have ever seen God, or they do not *really* know that they are loved, but they have stood at the ocean shore and marveled at its vastness. So invite them to dive into the expansive ocean-wide love of God. "Don't just dip your toes; get your hair wet!" So preach this, and people will know from their memories what you mean.

When an image works, it does not convince people of a truth. It sets them free to enter and explore a truth for themselves. It feels like you are telling them a bedtime story from childhood that they had long forgotten. In this sense, I think great preaching feels to listeners less like a classroom and more like a mother's lap—it is where you come to remember who you are, to be reminded that there is a Love that wants to swallow you up. Flaws and all, you are embraced.

If you think back on the books you have read that have meant the most to you, you will see a similar reality. The best books do not tell you something new. They give words and language and vocabulary to what you are already experiencing. They name what you already knew but were not yet able to articulate.

The best words make poetry out of the chaos, breathe *pneuma* onto the muck of life, not creating out of nothing, but creating with the raw material that is already inside of you. This is the sermon: not to teach but to tell what we all know or hope to know.

Henri Nouwen writes, "[Preaching is] the careful and sensitive articulation of what is happening in the community so that those who listen can say: 'You say what I suspected, you express what I vaguely felt, you bring to the fore what I fearfully kept in the back of my mind. Yes, yes—you say who we are, you recognize our condition . . . .'"[15]

To get to the bottom of things, to the bones of a matter, to the realness behind the veil, to the memory beneath the madness, we must undergo an *unlearning*, a stripping away, a certain sacred return to sparseness. We must create a graveyard for our illusions, a place where that which no longer serves us can die, a valley space where dry bones can collect. The shoot sprouts only after the seed falls into the ground and dies. Much of preaching is this sort of clearing work, taking us back to the bare bones, getting rid of accessories, garments, entrapments, and the like. The sermon carves out such a space by removing clutter, helping us unlearn what must be unlearned and release what must be released so that we can let go of arrogant or fear-driven assumptions about God and world and self.

Clarissa Pinkola Estés recounts the story of *La Loba*, an old woman who lives in a hidden place. Her sole work is collecting bones, recovering and preserving what is in danger of being lost to the world. She has a cave, and in it are bones of animals that she has hunted and brought back. She haunts the landscape, looking for bones. Once she has all the bones for a full skeleton of a wolf, or some other creature, she sets the skeleton out by the fire and thinks of a song to sing. When she knows the melody and the beginnings of words, she sings. She stands above the bones with raised arms, and she sings and she sings and she sings. The creature begins to take on fur, muscle, sinew, veins. It grows a tail. A heart begins to pump blood, and at last, the creature takes a breath. It stands on its feet, stretches its full body, then leaps and runs out into the wild, reborn.[16]

May we sift through this world, gathering bones, and then may we take the essence of our souls and with that essence make a song, and with that song, may life erupt.

"*Eternity is here already. Truth is not handed to you. It's in you already, more real than bone.*"[17]

The Contemplative Manifesto

Isaiah 60:1-6; Matthew 2:1-12
(Covenant Baptist Church, Epiphany Sunday)

We confess the lack of dreams. We have not the folly of wise men, who were open to the wonder of stars, ready to find God however long the journey, no matter if it led to a dirty stable. Reignite our imaginations, open our eyes, and energize our feet, that we might search, traverse, and pay homage.

We began our worship today with this prayer. There is not much we know concretely about the wise men. There is little we can say, much less prove, about their identities—who they were, where specifically they came from, what religion they adhered to, how long they'd been observing the skies, or why they put so much stock in this one astrological event. The one thing they are known for is following a star, a star that led them—unexpectedly, I presume—to a child of humble origin. And yet despite all the mystery that surrounds their arrival, I sense that we have a kinship with their journey.

Though they were Gentiles, it seems they must have known something of the Hebrew Scriptures, and so I wonder if these words from Isaiah were what woke them up in the night and prodded them to pack their bags: "Arise, shine, your light has come" (Isa 60:1). Was it Isaiah who provided the packing list? "They shall bring gold and frankincense and shall proclaim the praise of the LORD" (Isa 60:6).

Regarding our kinship with their journey, I wonder: When light enters your world, when the glory of the Lord shines upon you, will you arise? Or will you stay in bed? Will you follow the light of God wherever it leads, or will you sit tight? Will you share the light or hoard it?

I know it sometimes seems that light is in short supply. We have spoken before about waiting, waiting, waiting for the dawning of light after a dark night of the soul, but I have to wonder, at least about myself, if I ever get so desperate for sunrise that I grow bitter towards night and shut my eyes to the stars. I don't know how much darkness you live with, whether you are in a season of sun or whether you are in one of life's many waiting rooms. I don't know what the ratio of light to dark is for you at this time. I don't know how deep and wide and ravenous your craving for sunlight may be. But I know this: even before daybreak, there are stars. Even when it seems too black outside to see your own two feet in front of you, if you look up, there are tiny lights of guidance. Guidance for the journey. Guidance for the night's trek through foreign lands.

The writer Christina Baldwin says she wants to "move at the pace of guidance," and this is the wise man's pace, the wise woman's pace. The pace of guidance, I believe, is the mark of a true contemplative.

A contemplative doesn't exist just to contemplate. A contemplative contemplates and then moves according to the guidance, when the time is ripe, when he or she is called forward by a pinprick of Light. True contemplation is not merely sitting still. It is stillness in service of right action. Contemplative spirituality says, "Get out of the hamster-wheel religion that keeps you exerting energy in a sort of aimless desperation for fulfillment. Instead, lay out a blanket beneath the stars, sing and give thanks to the heavens for their expansiveness, and once you hear a light calling you forward, arise and move towards it."

For those still living in the land of darkness, don't worry so much about *when* the sun will break through the night. Take the light you have already been given and refract it back into the world like a prism or reflect it like a moon. You are not the Source or the Son, but there is light inside you all the same, and you have powerful shine. So arise. Shine.

The work of the contemplative is like the repetitive cleaning of a dingy, dusty mirror. You do not manipulate or coerce the light; light comes on its own. But you position yourself where the light can hit you, and you relentlessly, patiently, and gently keep removing the smudges life leaves on your ability to reflect the light. Arise. Shine.

Here is something you need to know: There will always be a Herod who tries to kill the thing you're after and sabotage the journey. This devil-in-disguise will sound like he has good motives; you will need to listen to your deeper wisdom, your dreams, your prayers, your heaven-sent messengers to know that he is a criminal. Once you start following Light, things will crop up to get in your way, to make you question your sanity, to challenge your resolve, to discourage your tenacity, and to slander your glow.

Every sojourner meets Herod. Every disciple gets the chance to be a wise man who spurns instruction or a Judas who gives in. Every Christ follower will be offered the chance to sell him out for thirty pieces of silver, precisely at the moment in your life when thirty measly dollars sounds like a fortune and the answer to all your problems. On your way to the child, you will stop at palaces where you will be tempted to make allies with the powers. You *will* meet resistance to your truest calling, and sometimes the resistance will sparkle at you like the promise of jewels. You won't always recognize the sinister right away, but it is never too late to alter your route to avoid further sabotage. You will make it past the resistance if you keep the echo of the call tucked close to your heart: "Arise, shine." It will never stop calling you to bypass the Herods and move towards the light.

We often say around here that we are a "contemplative Christian community," and we sometimes say right after that we aren't totally sure what we mean by those tongue-twisting words. In the spirit of Epiphany, I would like to suggest we mean this:

A contemplative isn't afraid of the shadows of life because he knows a shadow cannot be cast without light, doubt cannot be cast without faith, and sorrow cannot be cast without joy. The shadow means you are living in relation to light, doubt means you have a connection to faith, and sorrow means you have an equal capacity for joy. A contemplative is not afraid of the dark night because she knows that with the black night eventually comes the clarity and guidance of starlight. In the dead of night, something of the Spirit will make its way to her heart and show her where to go next.

Contemplatives are not afraid of long journeys—at least, not so afraid that they stay home. Contemplatives are not afraid of Herods, and they do not scoff at babies as divine presence. Contemplatives rarely scoff at anything, for that matter, because they remain so resolutely open to surprise, open to transformation, open to the power of changing one's mind when the signs so lead. Contemplatives are rarely too afraid of anything—they may *feel* a lot of fear because they are the type to let themselves feel things— but they do not fear to the point of cowering. They act in compliance with wisdom and love, never in subjection to angst.

Contemplatives cross boundaries. Like wise men traveling from east to west, contemplatives traverse a lot of territory, exhibit a willingness to befriend foreigners and a willingness to be foreigners in brand-new terrain. Contemplatives give extraordinary albeit unconventional gifts to the world. They keep a loose grip on their possessions and even their ideas. They are open to heading home by a different way if the angels so suggest.

Despite all the mystery surrounding the arrival of the wise men, I sense that we have a kinship to their journey. Maybe we are still a long way off from being contemplatives; maybe we are still on the patient lookout for guidance before we move; maybe there is still a dusty journey ahead of us. Even so, maybe you can hear the starlight whispering in your heart, "Arise. Shine," and maybe this is one of the years you will do so.

And so, though we may yet lack dreams, though we may have yet to attain the folly of wise men who were open to the wonder of stars, ready to find God however long the journey, we ask Thee, O Christ, to reignite our imaginations, open our eyes, and energize our feet that we might search, traverse, and pay homage. Amen.

The Locked Box

Luke 12:13-21 (Covenant Baptist Church)

Once upon a time, there was a little girl, and the little girl had a magic box, and the magic box held a great treasure, though the box was small. The box had been passed on to the girl from her grandfather when he died, and he had received it from his grandfather, who had received it from his great-uncle, and so on. It had been in the family for generations, so long, in fact, that no one quite remembered what precisely the treasure inside the box was, for it had not been opened in a very long time.

Throughout the family history, many feuds had erupted over who got the box next, as it passed without much rhyme or reason from one generation to the next. Sometimes to the firstborn, sometimes to the last born, sometimes to the son, sometimes to the daughter—the box was passed along to whomever the box so desired, but there was always much dissent among the children of the next generation as to whether the box had chosen wisely. It was even rumored that many years ago, blood had been shed in a duel for the box, but no matter what, the box always ended up where the box wanted. The fights continued, despite their futility.

When the little girl got the box, she was surprised, as no one expected the box to choose her. She was small and young and unaccomplished, and still the box bypassed all the more worthy members of the family and came to be in her possession. She treasured this box very, very much, for it was the only precious thing she'd ever owned. She set it high on a shelf in her room, and she admired it at length every night before she fell asleep.

One evening, while gazing at her box, she had an idea, and this idea was so moving that she did not sleep a wink the rest of the night. In the morning, she ran to her father right away. "Papa," she inquired, "I'd like to know: where's the key to my box?"

Her father started and raised his eyebrows. "The key? Why would you want the key?"

"Well, I was just thinking, I'd really like to *open* my box."

"*Open* your box? My dear, why would you need to *open* it? Isn't it enough that you *have* the box? Just *having the box* in your possession, why, that is so much more than most people in our family have been honored to do!"

The girl furrowed her brow. "Well, yes, I suppose so. But I just keep thinking, maybe the box *chose* me for a reason, and maybe I would better understand that reason if I could peek inside and know what I have."

Her father frowned. "The reason you have the box is to keep it safe until it is your turn to pass it on. That is how it has always been in our family, and you wouldn't want to mess with tradition now, would you?"

"No. No, I don't suppose I would want *that* . . . but still . . . ."

The girl sighed and retreated to her room. She took the box off the shelf and held it in her lap. She turned it round and round, examined the lock, shook it gently to see if she could hear anything inside. She was meant to open it; she just knew it. But how? She didn't know where to find a key, and *if* her father knew where the key was, he wasn't about to tell her.

"I know where the key is." The girl jumped at the voice. Her mother was standing at the doorway edge, peering in at her.

"You do?" She never expected her mother to know, seeing as how she had married into this family and its strange traditions. "How do you know and where is it and how could I get it?" she gushed all at once.

Her mother smiled. "I have always felt I was meant to help you open it, and so I've been doing some digging to find out about the key—it is the only way I am able to help you, being an outsider." Then her mother's face became grave. "But what I learned makes a mother's heart grow cold. The key is hidden far away, and you will have to embark on a long and dangerous journey to retrieve it."

"But I must go!" said the girl decidedly.

Her mother sighed. "I knew you would say that, if I told you. I am afraid for you, but I cannot go with you. It is a journey only the box-bearer can make. Are you sure you want to?"

The girl hesitated, but she already knew her answer. "Yes, I'm sure. This is why I was chosen."

"Yes, I believe you're right."

"Mother? I have another question. When was the last time the box-bearer tried to open the box?"

"I don't know. Many, many, many generations ago."

"Why has no one tried to open it since?"

"I don't know that either. I think perhaps your grandfather thought having the box on his shelf was nicer than facing the dangers of hunting down the key."

"Well, I disagree."

"Me too, my child. Me too."

And that was the beginning of the box-bearer's journey to find the key.

You know that drawer in your home where random stuff accumulates? The place where, among other things, you collect keys? Keys to old locks, keys that you can't remember what they go to, keys that you don't need often but just might need again. Eventually you've got so many keys that it's too daunting to ever pull them out because it would take hours to sort through and find out what goes where, but you're too afraid to throw them away in case something needs to be unlocked.

Well, imagine that the spiritual life is like sorting through a box of keys. It is slow and tedious work. But this is your Spiritual Work—not the shifting through keys per se, but the Unlocking of Locked Things. Spiritual life is this: unlocking your gratitude, unlocking your joy, unlocking your freedom, your talent, your capacity for love, unlocking your call, unlocking your inner spring, your true wisdom, your vivacious spirit. Unlock, unlock, unlock.

It's like this: God planted so many good things inside us when we were first formed by his hands, and yet evil came along and twisted things shut and added padlocks, and though by the grace of God we've been forgiven, it is a lifelong process to open ourselves back up. Sometimes we give up on the spiritual process of healing and opening because it feels as fruitless and time consuming as sorting through the junk drawer, looking for old keys to unlock lost treasures, but a nagging curiosity eventually draws us back to the work of sorting, unlocking, sorting, unlocking.

The vice of greed shuts this operation down. Greed is shutting the doors that were meant to swing open. Greed is tightening and closing and grasping and shutting and locking and hoarding and clutching—that is, taking the stuff that was meant to be gift and breath to us and fearfully squeezing the life out of it.

So this man approaches Jesus and wants Jesus to tell his brother to give him part of the inheritance. Jesus is a man of justice; surely he can arbitrate. You can almost hear Jesus sigh; this is not what the kingdom is about. But with Jesus, no one's question is ever dismissed. Everything you could think to say to Jesus—self-centered or distracted or misplaced as it might be—he's ready to open up an opportunity for you to learn. And that's what he did with this man. He looked him in the eye and said, let me tell you a story about a rich man.

Only it's a pretty boring story. The man is rich. He gets richer when his crops do well. So he plans to build some big barns to store the grain. And once it is stored, then he'll know he's set for life, and he can sit back, relax, and enjoy life. So, basically, it's as if I were to tell you, Once upon a time, a middle-class man was doing fairly well for himself, and one year he did even better than usual, and he thought to himself, "I'm going to open a retirement account, and once I have ample goods laid up for many years, I will finally relax, eat, drink, and be merry."

See what I mean? This is hardly a story. It's just a description of our lives. In essence, it's retirement planning, against which there are no laws or commandments that I'm aware of. In fact, it's what the responsible people do; they plan ahead. This is the kind of man who would make my parents proud. Then comes the twist in the story. "You fool!" says God to the man, which is startling for me, and for some reason I think of Gandalf right before he goes plummeting off the cliff with the Balrog in *The Fellowship of the Ring*: "Fly, you fools!"

That seems a little dramatic for this ordinary, average, just-like-everybody-else man's life. It turns out the man's about to die, so I guess that is a little bit dramatic. But we didn't see it coming. You're never thinking about an early death when you're planning for retirement. You're planning for a long life, and surely there's nothing foolish about that, unless, of course, you're about to die and your last day would have been better spent playing with the children rather than balancing the books, but who can predict that?

So what's Jesus' point? Never make plans? "Take care! Be on your guard against all kinds of greed," are Jesus' exact words and this brings us right back to the whole business of clutching versus opening, locking versus unlocking. Here's a man who has been blessed, and he wants to lock his blessings in a barn, and when his stuff outgrows the barn and threatens to spill over, he'll just tear up that barn and build a bigger one. Can't have grain peeking out the crevices, can we? *That* might start to feel like abundance, if you can see the excess, and that's the thing greed hates the most: for you *to notice* how much you have. Bigger barns, bigger storage units, bigger houses, bigger closets—these help to hide the truth of what you have so you can keep feeling panicky about what you don't have or what you might lose if you don't hold on tight enough.

Greed is not just about money and possessions, by the way, though those things can certainly trip you up. Greed is any time we hold on too tight. It's any time we believe the lie that there isn't enough. It's any time we shut the door on trust. It's any time we operate out of fear of the future rather than with a sense of adventure. It's like we keep passing locked boxes on from one generation to the next and never opening them. We're too afraid to take a real peek, to enjoy what we've been given.

I've been reading a book called *Daring Greatly* by Brené Brown, and she writes about the discomfort of what she calls "foreboding joy," that is, how joy makes us vulnerable because we grow afraid that the joy means we're about to face loss. Have you ever felt this way? Often we use the phrase "too good to be true" because we know something bad is bound to happen. Maybe we even lower our expectations in life so as to save ourselves the disappointment. Brené interviewed one man who said he used to think the best way to live life was to expect the worst—that way, if the worst happened, you were prepared; if it didn't happen, you could be pleasantly surprised. Then his wife died in a car accident, and he realized that expecting the worst didn't prepare him at all. Now he grieves all the wonderful moments he shared with her but didn't really enjoy because he was "preparing." His new commitment to her, even now that she's gone, is to fully enjoy each moment. No one can avoid, or even prepare for, tragedy. In her research, Brené discovered that the way to face the vulnerability of joy and have the courage to embrace the joy anyway, despite its uncertainty, is to practice gratitude. Not to *feel* grateful, but to have actual concrete practices in your life that help you pause and be grateful. When she interviewed people who had endured horrific tragedies, gratitude was one thing she discovered as a common denominator among them. After facing the worst, they had learned to slow down and appreciate what they had.[18]

It's amazing how the gifts we've been given can make us feel vulnerable; we want to lock our kids, our spouses, our parents, our homes in a great big barn where nothing and no one can get hurt. We think we're being safe, but Jesus says, "Watch out! Be on your guard" against such behaviors, because eventually you'll stop being capable of enjoying what is in front of you.

Where greed is concerned, here's the key that fits the lock: gratitude. Practicing gratitude is the key that unlocks your box, your barn, and the safety deposit box where you've foolishly stowed your joy. Sometimes gratitude feels like the labored first steps of a long journey towards wholeness. Other times, certain moments of gratitude are downright powerful enough to smash those greed locks to bits.

When the little girl embarks on her journey to find the key to unlock her box, we don't know whether she's going to make it back. We don't know what dangers, what obstacles, what setbacks she'll encounter. All we know is that she decides it is worth it to risk it, to risk the unknown rather than adhere to the tradition of safely preserving the box but never opening it.

You've been given life, a great gift from God. You can use that life, live it, open it up, share it with the world. Or you can build a big practical barn and save your life for a rainy day. You can set your box on a shelf in the bedroom and admire it. Or you can set out to find the key. No one knows if you will return when you do. No one knows what dangers, what obstacles, what setbacks you may encounter. It's a story that doesn't yet have an ending. But you get to choose whether it is worth it to risk disappointment that you might know delight, to risk heartache that you might know a full heart.

I recommend this: Live. Unlock. Let go. Give thanks. Fly, you fools. Amen.

8

gut:
intuition in preaching

í cuRRentlʸ feel scammeɒ by God. We are still working through it, he and I. (I've noticed I call God *he* when I feel upset with him. Go figure.) Has this ever happened to you, or am I the only one with this much confusion and this little faith?

I (rather bravely in my estimation) followed a path I thought God was beckoning me down. These steps required a lot of trust, and leaping out in faith like that made me feel close to God, like the two of us were tight, like I *heard* things from God that people don't usually hear. I was in the God-zone, the God light. Only . . . .

It turned out to be the wrong path.

How did I know it was wrong? Because a door slammed in my face, blocking the path, and no matter how hard and how long I knocked, it did not reopen.

I am still trying to sort this one out, and I feel this would be a *much* better essay for my readers if I could just understand it in its entirety and tell you neatly how it is. Instead, I have some theories:

One is that God never lied to me—I just misheard him. (Notice the pronoun; I'm still upset.) The problem with theory number one is if it turns out I am *that bad* at hearing God, then I I might as well give up.

Another theory is that I did hear God right, but I heard God *early* somehow, and the path will become clear, if only I stay patient. The problem with that theory is that I am running out of patience. It feels like a carrot-at-the-end-of-a-stick situation in which I'm the donkey. It seems as though I will keep pursuing but never reach that carrot.

Another theory is that I *sorta* heard God right, but I somehow got the details mixed up a bit and it will sort itself out in time if I just keep listening. The problem with that theory is it is damn aggravating.

If I'm going to be honest, I have to admit I feel that God lied to me. Tricked me. Seduced me. Whether or not this matches reality may be another matter, but that is how I feel.

This would be an irksome situation for anyone who wants to maintain some sort of faith in God, but it is an especially weighty burden for a minister. It is an even heavier burden for a girl, who, over time, has made a pact with God that she will go whichever way God nudges, no matter how unconventional or nonconformist, as long as God makes clear-ish the nudge.

I am not looking for sympathy; I'm just explaining how much it throws me out of sync when God lies to me. I have spent the majority of my life obeying clear-ish nudges, some murkier than others, and so far, as best I can tell, these nudges have led me to the right path, even when I didn't understand what I was doing at the time.

I'm not always comfortable assigning such nudges to God. I mean, these so-called nudges could come from my reasoning skills or my emotions. The promptings could merely be the result of impatience, indigestion, or irritation. But on some occasions I really can sense something holy and Other-than-myself at play. Other times, I am less sure, but I still suspect the divine is speaking to me. It seems presumptuous to call it God every time. The "still small voice" label works for me though. "Still small voice" suggests something quiet, suggests something *almost* out of hearing, suggests a voice you could easily mistake for something less powerful and less worth your time, suggests it is so small and still, you might even misunderstand what it is saying, so you have to be cautious about claiming what you've heard as truth. However, when I follow the still, small voice over time I can see how that seemingly insignificant nudge was, in fact, the voice of God. My shorthand name for that still, small voice is *intuition*.

I suspect intuition is the most wounded element of our preaching (not to mention our living). I believe our faith in intuition needs revitalizing and healing and restoration. Intuition shrivels when we fail to honor it within ourselves.

Generally speaking, we don't trust it. Like blaming Eve, we blame intuition for things gone awry. Better to trust books, facts, rules, tradition, external authority. What is being spoken to you from within might be (must be?) a deceiver.

Certainly we all have lies floating through our minds that need to be sifted through, sorted, and disposed of where necessary. We are all capable of being wrong—even when we feel passionately right—but falsehoods do not originate in our intuition. Falseness arises from our small self, from our shadow, and from the negative outer voices we have internalized. Sometimes outer voices are so familiar they sound like our own; they shape us and continue to play in our minds like old tapes we can't shut off. But these harmful voices have nothing to do with our intuition. They are enemies of intuition.

Our intuition is a pure, inner knowing. Untainted by darkness, she is a beam of light that can cut through confusion and tell us the truth or guide us about what to do.

She is the voice that speaks to us about our decisions on a level deeper than our pros and cons lists, deeper than what we can figure out mathematically or scientifically, deeper than what we can read in a book. Intuition is where the Holy Spirit speaks clearly in a way we can discern. She is where Peace greets us and inexplicable Vision pierces us. She is where we can hear the still, small voice of God. Intuition is where the divine spark resides, where the *imago dei* is preserved with integrity. She is the place in our hearts that feels like coming home, where the stream flows clear and uncontaminated. She is where we hear messages that we wouldn't be open to hearing any other way. She is where we are inspired and where we are caught up in a certain way of being and where Love is the overwhelming presence. She is where empathy originates, where healing sprouts, and where art is created.

We live in a world dominated by facts and figures. The gypsy wanderer voice of our intuition is rarely welcome. The wisdom she offers is not based on research you can footnote, but that is her beauty: she is truly original.

Many of us are so removed from our intuition that we don't recognize her when she speaks. Intuition has a quiet voice, but sometimes she has to scream to get our attention (like the terrible stomachache you get while making a bad decision) until we finally listen and choose differently. We constantly beat our intuition into silence, second-guess her, mock her, stop up our ears. We secretly fear her. We fear she might go wild if we let her loose because the truth is that intuition does not politely follow convention, toe the party line, or promote efficiency. Intuition often whispers truths in our ears that we did not want to know. She can turn us topsy-turvy. She can turn us into real radicals and she can keep our ambitions modest. This is alarming business, and no wonder we have shunned her, our deepest knowing.

But this is the place inside us where gospel explodes into a living, breathing, pulsating thing with a life of its own. It is good news that cannot be contained, that does not always play well with others, has a stripe of feisty and a penchant for the unexpected. As Richard Rohr says, saints who live out of their true self are always free to obey, but they might also disobey.[19]

Intuition: this is where our rebel selves are birthed. I do not mean rebel for the sake of rebelling. I mean true freedom-in-Christ as a real force in our lives, guiding us hither and thither by the wind of the Spirit without respect for the expectations of others. What the biblical writers call "freedom in Christ" is not the freedom to do whatever you want without regard for others. Instead, it is the freedom to follow the Spirit, the freedom to cross fences, the freedom to live large in service of Love.

This intuition-inspired freedom is what prompts the missionary to sell her comfortable home and move halfway across the world. This is the spark that inspires a father to turn down a promotion to have more time with his family or the gumption that motivates a stay-at-home mom to pursue her dream even though it will require some daycare time for the children. This is the voice that tells us to say "no" to things that otherwise look promising and "yes" to things that otherwise look all wrong. It is what inspires the artist to paint and the musician to compose and the poet to write and the dancer to move her body. Intuition is what gets an ordinary person suddenly to notice his untamable imagination, like a bear waking from hibernation. It is what causes someone well past middle life to suddenly twinkle with renewed energy and reclaim the adventure of living before it is too late.

For me, all the best decisions I have made would never have happened had I stuck to reason alone. My most rewarding ventures have always been driven by something I could not quite explain. My most important decisions have been ones I couldn't entirely defend.

The energy that intuition generates is absolutely essential to preaching because Scripture is a living text. Commentaries and study are not enough to tap its mysteries. You must know how to listen to the depths beneath the depths if you are to hear the Scriptures speak. You must be awake to your intuitive guides, must be alert to Spirit, must be in tune to the still, small voice. You must have given up condemning her, otherwise you will keep shutting her out every time she tries to travel off-route from your certainties. It will never serve you well to silence her. You must, must, must let her speak.

In my experience, most of the things my intuition speaks to me are very small: make a phone call, send an e-mail, breathe a teensy prayer, get up from my desk and take a walk, pull out my journal and write down the phrase rattling around in my mind. It's not as if I look for writing in the sky or dramatic signs in the universe. We often *want* to hear an obvious voice that could tell us what to do, particularly when we are in distress, but intuition isn't like that. It is the very soft voice inside ourselves. When we are desperate for something big to point the way as clearly as a billboard, we might hear a whisper in our hearts that says, "Take a bubble bath," or "Call your mom," and we will think, *What the hell? I wanted to hear something helpful.* But all those small whispers, if honored, build up to a vibrant, awake life. One day we will discover that all those seemingly silly disjointed little lines created poetry out our lives. In some probably imperceptible way, by listening to her we have changed the world, or at least we have changed ourselves.

But when your intuition fails you and seems to have driven you down the wrong path—what then? I am still sorting that one out, but I have seen enough to know I mustn't give up on her. I am tempted to believe there are no wrong paths where intuition is concerned, only necessary detours whereby we learn things we may have never encountered any other way. But let me tell you, finding out you've been on a detour does not feel holy, guided, helpful, or instructive. It feels like shit.

It takes a lifetime to hone your listening skills, to figure out how to keep trusting, keep following, even though the path is winding and at times downright confusing.

Furthermore, intuition is not safe. It does not keep you from failing or misunderstanding or hurting. Intuition does not stop bad things from happening to you. Even when you take the right path, there are still obstacles, tragedies, and hardships along the way. If something goes wrong, it doesn't mean you heard God wrong. Intuition is a guide, not a bodyguard. It can lead you through the forest, tell you where to turn, but it cannot stop the forest from having grizzly bears.

A life listening to God is never boring and never certain. I consistently get confused. I am consistently surprised. I am consistently stretched, and I consistently learn more than I knew yesterday. There are long stints in the dark, and there are sunrises. No matter how many times it feels like it all might be a scam, I've decided I'll take my chances.

True Repentance

Joel 2:12-15 (Ash Wednesday,
Covenant Baptist Church)

"Remember that you are dust and to dust you shall return." And remember that between being dust and becoming dust again, you are a sparkling gem of God's own making; you are a shimmering creation meant to light up some small corner of earth. Between dust and dust, you were made to live, and this is the task set before you, not to waste a life but to fill a life. Between dusts is a short span, but it is a long enough span to find your purpose and follow it.

Repentance is the thing with wings that carries you into new life and new horizons. Repentance isn't a dirty word or a sad one or a punitive one or a dismal one. Repentance is the happy thing that sets you alive, that reminds you to sparkle as long as you've still got breath in you. Somehow, amazingly, God took the dust of you, stirred it with energy, breathed into it God's own wind, pumped your veins with blood and your brain with ideas and your bones with strength and your flesh with muscle, and all of this is a miracle you do no want to throw away.

This is the objective of repentance: to return you back to life in God. To recall to your consciousness your aliveness. To remind you of your worth so that you will stop doing things that are unworthy of your time and your energy, things that are unworthy of a gem like you.

One year for Lent I tried to re-add the practice of confession into my life while simultaneously giving up negative thoughts about myself. These two practices seemed contradictory at first because, when I was growing up, confession was always about the bad stuff, my yucky parts being exposed. To confess was to think poorly of one's sinful self.

But genuine confession is ultimately a declaration of the good. Yes, we admit to the shadowy parts of our egos; we confess our addictions, our grasping, our whining, our obsessions. We confess all the ways we have been living less than we are meant to live, and we confess all the places in our lives where fear still has its hold on us.

But more than that, we confess the Love that is bigger than all of it. We confess the Life we really want to live in Christ. We confess that small living need not confine us or constrain us anymore. We confess our belief in abundance. We confess our belief in mercy. We confess that we are being carried by a Beauty stronger than our puniest deficiencies. We confess that, oh yes, now I remember: the lap of God is better and safer and warmer than all the cold, measly idols I have surrounded myself with for protection and comfort.

Scott Cairns says repentance is when we realize that our sin is not so bad as it is a waste of time.[20] When you are stuck repeating the same old patterns that get you nowhere, repentance is the light beam, the mercy, the joy that intersects your path and suddenly opens a new way forward. When you are wedged in a hard place, trying the same old methods to no avail, repentance is the creative insight that bursts through rock and concrete. Repentance is when suddenly there is a doorway where you thought there was only solid wall. Repentance is when the still, small voice whispers inside your heart, "Come this way," while your fear is saying, "But everyone else is going that way." It is when your heart presses on and says, "Trust me. Come this way." Repentance is when you finally get brave enough to try something new. Repentance is when you finally find the gumption to move this way instead of that. Repentance is when God calls, and praise be to heaven, this time you hear him and recognize it as a Word meant for your soul.

In Scripture, when a person repents, the heavens erupt in a party. That's because repentance is joy and life and light and love and power and *relief* that finally God spoke, or finally you are listening, or finally you understand, or finally you have just enough hutzpah to take the first step in a new direction.

You don't really have to work at repentance. Repentance finds you if you are listening for it. If you are willing to take the journey, it will meet you on the road.

I invite you in the stillness that follows this homily to write about what repentance might mean for you this season. If you don't yet know what repentance looks like, then write about your stuck places. Where in your life are you spinning your wheels? What is draining lifeblood from you? Where do you need the light of repentance to crack through the wall and show you a way forward?

This Lenten season, may we find the voice of God amid the scurry of our lives. May repentance grip us with clarity and wisdom. May we find the thing God is saying to our hearts. May we find the pathway the Spirit is opening up before us. May we find the love Christ is looking to plant within us. May we quiet ourselves, hear the Wind blow its stirring, creative breaths, and then let it carry us to new places, like dust dancing with God-force.

May we, this day, renew the journey of repentance. Whatever parts of our lives feel burnt up of their energy, may God stir the ashes and set us on course yet again.

Amen.

Where Is Lady Wisdom?

Proverbs 1:20-33a (Covenant Baptist Church)

She started out front and center, right in the throbbing heart of the city. Her voice rang boldly in the public square. She beckoned and she persuaded, poured all her heart and beauty and passion into pleading words, offered without discrepancy holy gifts and invaluable teaching, and gave it all away for free to poor and rich alike. But the townspeople loved their own ways and didn't like having her there to interrupt and distract. So they kicked her out. Shut down her voice and stopped up their ears. Spurned her, ignored her, threw stones, and drove her out.

She let them drive her away. She did not lose her spirit, for no one could rob her of that, but she left town and took her spirit and her gifts with her. She kept watch over the city from a hilltop far away and laughed when they began to miss her. She played hide and seek with the few brave souls who ventured out to find her again. She knew they only half-wanted her, and while she'd always been bold and gracious, she'd never been easy or cheap, and thus she remained evasive, though never entirely lost.

Today's story recounts the departure of Lady Wisdom.

When I read these first few verses about Wisdom calling aloud out in the open, raising her voice in the public square, crying out from a busy street corner, making speeches from the city gate, I am perplexed. Every time I have ever wanted to make a wise decision, I have had to search long and hard. I have had to hunt to find Wisdom, wrestle back the monsters of my ego to free her. In my experience, it is hard work to uncover wisdom. And here she is in the book of Proverbs, just as open and accessible, loud and obvious as can be. Why can't she *shout* into my life like that, so that I don't have to work so hard to hear her?

She doesn't cry aloud anymore because we silenced her! Plain and simple, that's what the story tells us. We shut Wisdom up (or at least refused to listen), and she carried her voice elsewhere, and with her departure, distress struck our wisdom-voided world.

That's how the book of Proverbs begins: exhorting us to gain Wisdom, warning us that Wisdom is elusive, and reminding us it is our own fault that she went into hiding in the first place.

People like the book of Proverbs for its concise advice—chapter after chapter, you'll find verse after verse you could crochet on a pillow. But the proverbs are not sound bytes to save for a rainy day. They are not tricks for success when the going gets rough. They are not Post-it notes to keep us on track. The proverbs are breadcrumbs on the trail to find Wisdom. One saying alone isn't enough for nourishment; it's the trail that matters, the pursuit, the movement deeper and deeper and deeper. We aren't after clever morsels; we're after Wisdom, and she cannot be invoked with a pretty phrase. But she can be followed if we observe the trail.

It's not surprising that Wisdom is hard to come by; we've learned that much from life experience. The startling thing in this poem is to find out that Wisdom is, in fact, a bit saucy. We spurn her, she spurns us. We quit listening, she quits talking, or at least, she directs her speech elsewhere.

And Wisdom laughs, *laughs* at our distress. I do not envision Wisdom laughing spitefully with a Cruella de Vil cackle, as if she delighted in evil. I imagine instead the amused laugh of a free spirit, of one who knows there is a fullness to life beyond the limitedness to which we constrain ourselves by rebuking her wisdom. She's not caught up in our systems and games and power struggles, so she smiles broadly when we get stumped by our own constructs. Wisdom weeps too, of course, for the ones who get trampled through no fault of their own. But she laughs when the tramplers get tripped; our tragedies are her comedy, as fate is so often in her favor, willing us to acknowledge that we are lost without her wisdom. She won't make us listen to her words or her logic, but her spunk isn't so easily ignored. Her spirited passion is a force to be reckoned with, even after we've kicked her out of town.

We see in this poem that Lady Wisdom starts out full of invitation and promise, but by the end of the poem she is aloof and mysterious, distant, willingly secretive. And the book of Proverbs poses this question to us: Will you go looking for her?

There are plenty of wisdom parodies parading around town, smug in her absence. Lots of people settle for these fakers with their easy, quick answers, flashy clichés, and popular promises of prosperity. Some townspeople recognize this fraudulent wisdom for the sham that it is and expend all their energy trying to drive those goons out or at least make people quit listening to them.

Only a rare few pack their bags and set out on foot to find the real Her. Even fewer keep up the chase when they realize how much of a maze it is out there and how long (a lifetime, they say) it will take to find her.

But what the longtime Wisdom seekers will tell you is that, although you never quite lay hold of her like a prize or manage to snatch her up for your own consumption, the longer you seek, the more readily you spot her. Your tracking abilities improve, of course, but at times you'll swear she sought you out to whisper her secrets to the wind, just close enough for you to overhear. Sometimes she'll linger, right in your line of vision, long enough for you to gaze, to shudder, to transform.

They even say that sometimes Wisdom dances right back through the middle of town, though she always wears a disguise. Sometimes she dresses up like a beggar, other times as a child. There's a glint in her eye that she cannot hide, and the few who catch her eye stop in their tracks and repent. Most everyone drives her back out of town without knowing who she really is, or they simply ignore her altogether.

One time, she came in the form of a carpenter's boy from Nazareth, the scandalous son of an unwed mother, and that time it was just *too much*, and the townspeople called for a killing and drug him to a hill. "Father, forgive them, for they do not know what they are doing," cried Wisdom. Legend has it that, though the brutality was fearsome that day, Wisdom lived on.

To this day, she can still be spotted, drifting in forgotten places, sharing melodies with the children, flitting here and there like spirit. Those who listen to her live in safety, without fear, like a child in a mother's arms. It is no child's play, though, this safety, because Wisdom often demands that you do dangerous deeds just because it's the right thing to do. But she does provide the distinct kind of safety that comes from having a bit of her spunk, a bit of her insight, a bit of courage planted inside you.

I wrote a tribute to Lady Wisdom, and I would like to share it with you.

Townsmen ordered exile,
She became elusive,
a wanderer traversing earth,
a noble nomad harboring
her vagabond truth:

Now in sly seclusion,
by regal irreverence
She keeps watch
Crops fail:
She laughs
and plucks a wild berry.
She dances in moonlight,
Disappears behind trees
Like a spirit
You cannot catch her
Like the wind
She is free
A rare gift is to sight her,
rarer still to hear her sing
Her music is forever
in the woods and in the wind,
harked by birds and forest creatures
overheard by pure of heart,
by seekers and by drifters,
ears bursting from constraint.

She is subtle
if she shows herself—
You can find her in a painting,
In a poem, in the starlight
In wildflower petals
In lines of holy writ
At times beneath steeples

Inside a mother's arms
Most of all in silence
Her gentle whisper
Roars
Like on the rooftop
She cries loudly,
Beckons boldly
If you'll listen
If you'll follow
Wisdom calls.

Amen.

veins:
emotion in preaching

ƒeelings. Uck. too much, too many, too manipulative. I, for one, have always preferred logic and reason as the tidier companions. Feelings are what I stuff in the back of the closet where guests cannot see. They collect in my junk drawers in piled-up jumbles, threatening to spill over and out into the open, but I am consistent at shutting doors and keeping cabinets closed, even when I'm home alone. The mess of them makes me uncomfortable and uneasy. Feelings make me seem out of control, as if I have ceased to be a restful home to myself. Feelings suggest that I am all in disarray, unfit for company, even my own.

Fighting my emotions, I once wrote in a blog post, "So intensely do I wish to escape this season of sorrow, be finished with grief, close it up in a box and take it to the attic, then climb down the rickety steps to a happy home and forget all about it." And it is not only the negative emotions like grief and sadness and anxiety that I wish to shut out. I often find all feeling a little threatening. You never know when unshackled joy might sneak up and seduce you to act out of character. I am much too sophisticated to *feel* things. I am above all that emotional stuff.

In all honesty, I always have been a person of mild temperament. My mother tells me that when I was a toddler, they could never tell by my expression if I liked something. "Do you want to do that again?" they would ask. If I said, "Yes," that meant I was enjoying myself. If I said, "No," that meant I was anywhere from bored to disgusted. In any case, my facial cues and my tone of voice remained essentially the same. (Someone should have caught on and taught me how to play poker.) Eventually I picked up non-verbal communication skills, but expressing myself emotionally has always been a challenge.

I am also someone with delayed emotional reactions. As a result, people often perceive me as calm, patient, and self-controlled, but the truth is that I cannot help it. It is not that I am resisting the urge to curse and yell; it is that I do not feel the anger and frustration until I walk away. In the moment, my feelings often stay hidden, frozen in some corner to which I banished them, I suppose, and then they visit me later, when it is safe to make an appearance.

I have been this way for as long as I can remember. I dislike shouting, angry outbursts, and dramatic shows of emotion. When I am around overt, loud emotion, I tend to withdraw and grow quiet and stoic. Sometimes if a family member I deeply love acts over-the-top excited to see me, I involuntarily shut down because I am overwhelmed, trying to both process all that emotion and reciprocate appropriately as expected.

I am not so much trying to portray myself as cold and robotic as to explain that it took me an extended effort to learn how to feel my feelings, how to let them into my front room, how to give them a seat in my easy chair. Nowadays (and somewhat surprisingly) I write a lot about feelings, first as a way to process what I struggle to admit belongs to me, and second to make it up to my heart for such long negligence.

Sometimes I tell bits of my life to my friend Aurelia, who is more healthily emotive than I, just to find out how I am supposed to feel. She reacts to my life quicker than I do, and it helps. She names with lightning speed what I am trying to feel way down deep somewhere, and it allows me to say, "Oh! There you are, Anger. Hello, Excitement. I recognize you now, Apprehension."

Growing up in an unfortunately still-sexist environment, I heard it repeatedly declared that women wouldn't/couldn't make good presidents, CEOs, community leaders, etc. because women are too emotional. Emotions get in the woman's way of making good decisions and prevent her from being objective. I internalized this message. Even though I was already less outwardly emotional than just about any of my friends, male or female, I still believed it would be a weakness if I ever let those feelings seep out. I was as smart as my male colleagues, and I was determined never to let something as silly and fickle as *feelings* thwart my capacity to reason with the best of them.

Even on the basketball court, I was the model of good sportsmanship. In over six years of competitive ball, I don't recall ever losing my cool and throwing an elbow. Even my athletic aggression stayed within bounds. I could play an entire game, secure points, steals, assists, and rebounds, and walk away without a single foul to my name. I was abnormally controlled.

One day in high school basketball practice, however, I got genuinely pissed. We were scrimmaging against one another, and repeatedly the other team was scoring on fast breaks after the defensive rebound. For some reason, my team was lagging behind all day, and over and over again I was the only one hustling back on defense, left alone to try to stop three or more offensive players. It was unusual for my teammates to play with so little fervor, and I grew increasingly frustrated at their lazy response. "Get back on defense!" I kept shouting to no avail.

Finally, I had enough. I was bringing the ball up the court after yet another easy lay up by the opposing team. I picked up my dribble, froze icily just past half court, making it clear with my body that the play would not continue until I said so. "Whose girl is that?" I demanded ferociously, pointing to the person who kept scoring. No one answered. I did not budge. "Whose girl is that?" I repeated, and by now I was shouting passionately. A wide-eyed teammate fearfully raised her hand in admission, "She's mine."

I glared at her with death in my eyes. "Then you better get back on defense." It was clearly a command. At the next fast break, I scanned the court and zeroed in on the confessing slacker. She was, yet again, jogging half-heartedly down the floor. I raced towards her, placed my palm firmly on her back and shoved her forward with force. As hard as I could, I shoved. I shoved, and she ran. In fact, she ran faster than I'd ever seen her run before.

After practice ended, I could scarcely believe myself, screaming in a rage at my own teammates, even *shoving* one of them. This was not the collected Kyndall most people were accustomed to. This was not the supportive, motivational point guard I was used to being. I felt guilty.

Coach Jim pulled me aside. "Great job today," he said. I blinked in disbelief. "That's exactly the kind of leadership we need from our senior captain," he told me, patting my shoulder. "I want to see more of that." I was shocked. His words were a challenge to my entire polished persona, and I struggled with whether I was hearing him right. *Was he really suggesting that my emotional outburst was good and helpful to my team?* I have never forgotten the day Coach Jim applauded my anger.

I wish I could say that's the moment when I learned to let emotion in and let emotion out. But it was another decade before Coach Jim's affirmation took root. The final straw came much later. For me, it was slamming up against a terrible grief that finally cracked the dam. Fissure by fissure, emotions began to leak out.

The real breaking point came the week I made the toughest decision of my life, and two days after that, I received some of the worst news of my life, and the day after that, I was hidden away at a Benedictine retreat center, wondering how I was going to cope with so much alone time with such roaring emotions for company. I have never in my life had to face as much rage or hurt as I had to face in that place. I had this sense when I entered my little hermitage for the week: either being on retreat right after disaster was the best place to be, or the solitude was going to be hell. Like most monastic settings, my room was sparse, but hanging on the wall was a poem. It was the only poem in the room. The poem was "The Guest House" by Rumi, and it said,

> This being human is a guest house.
> Every morning a new arrival.
> A joy, a depression, a meanness,
> some momentary awareness
> comes as an unexpected visitor.
>
> Welcome and entertain them all!
> Even if they are a crowd of sorrows,
> who violently sweep your house
> empty of its furniture,
> still, treat each guest honorably.
> He may be clearing you out
> for some new delight.

The dark thought, the shame, the malice.
meet them at the door laughing and invite them in.

Be grateful for whatever comes.
because each has been sent
as a guide from beyond.[21]

I am not hugely confident that I receive signs from God, but if ever I got a sign, that was one. After reading "The Guest House," I began to write profusely about emotions. I wrote letters to my rage, to my grief, to my hurt, and to my confusion. I let everything in, and then I also let it out on the opened page of my journal. I told a few people what I was dealing with, I spent loads of time outdoors, and I found as many tiny ways to be gentle to myself as I could muster. But mostly I wrote poetry, and to this day I can attest that the single most helpful thing that has seen me through terror is writing.

All of this is not to say, "Be emotive when you preach," because who needs to be told that no one likes monotone speakers? What I am telling you is that, like them or not, feelings are a part of your life, and if you do not extend hospitality even to the darker and more intense among them, your sterile home will not have much to offer the world.

Emotions will mess you up.

Let them.

The point is not to be dominated by emotional reactions—that will get you into trouble. But do not swing the pendulum to the other extreme and try to exercise dominion over your feelings to keep them in check. You must *befriend* your emotions, let them out of the closet, learn to harmonize with a messy roommate.

You have to pay close attention. Feelings do not always tell the truth, and so you will want to remain open to discernment as you let yourself feel. But ignoring them only aggravates their exaggerative powers. You are being asked to heed what they are speaking to you. Emotions are teachers, albeit wild ones. If treated with compassionate openness, they will lead you to empathy, insight, and passion. If treated with disdain and attempts at control, they will close your heart and haunt your dreams.

Even the darker, uncomfortable feelings lead to good things if you keep the door to your heart swinging open. You must let the dark stuff in, feed it dinner even, but you must not hold it hostage. When the anger and such is ready to leave, you must let it go. Don't hold on—that is bad roommate etiquette. The loving home/heart welcomes without reservation and says good-bye without grasping.

Stay open. Feel. Stretch. Expand. Whatever comes your way, don't close up. Do not control. Be. Sit with all of it. Lay down with your sorrow. Make love.

Erotic Song, Sacred Text

Song of Songs 2:8-13 (Covenant Baptist Church)

There is perhaps no book of the Bible so enigmatic as the Song of Songs. Not only are its authorship and purpose mysterious, but the whole song is downright indiscreet. *If* you read it at all, you probably read it in secret. It's the kind of poetry that's challenging to read in church without blushing, like opening to a nude painting in your *school* textbook of all places. We expect certain texts to be censored and sanitized, and the disorientation of finding one not so can be a little embarrassing.

Of course, throughout the centuries, the church has done its best to make Song of Songs a book about *God*, about God's love for God's people and the people's love for God. It's the interpretation we would expect, but interestingly the *name of God* does not appear even once in all eight chapters. For this reason and many others, the book continues to cause readers and scholars to scratch their heads or even flush pink as they read.

For example, the name *Solomon* appears a handful of times, first in the title, which reads in Hebrew, "The Song of Songs, which is Solomon's." But while the phrase "which is Solomon's" *could mean* written by Solomon, it could just as easily mean written *about* Solomon, written *for* Solomon, written *in the style of* Solomon, etc. The real author of the song is virtually unknown, with no solid evidence to bolster a single theory.

The most likely scenario is that the writer of the Song of Songs was a woman, because if you pay attention, the dominant speaker is a woman's voice and the story is predominately portrayed from a woman's perspective. The male speaker has few lines compared to the women, and the notion that Solomon penned these words is almost surely myth.

I also doubt the poet was in love with the real King Solomon. If you consider Solomon and his hefty harem of women, you can hardly imagine that he experienced the kind of intense, exclusive, and mutual love we read about in the poem. The scattered references to Solomon that appear in the song are likely the wordplay of the writer. She uses linguistic resourcefulness as she poetically likens her lover to a wealthy, wise king by invoking the name of Solomon.

Whoever the author and whoever her subject, this poem is a shockingly, refreshingly different kind of voice in Scripture: its distinctly feminine tone, its unashamed awe of the human body—both male and female—its unapologetic portrayal of human desire, its poetic and enigmatic references, its playful spirit coupled with its burning passion, its undeniable reverence for the wonder of creation, its puzzling lack of any reference to YHWH.

It is just enough of a scandal to make a person wonder what makes this book *Scripture*, exactly? Why was this specific collection of writings chosen to belong to our canon? Why include love poetry that flirts with the erotic? It is the gypsy text of Scripture, and while *our* prudish sensibilities might advise that we leave it out, some time ago the Holy Spirit confided in the hearts of men such that they refused to ostracize this story for its lack of propriety and instead embraced these words as sacred and holy text.

From the beginning, this poem has been interpreted allegorically, or more accurately, interpreted in the spiritual sense. The intense relationship between two lovers depicted in the poem serves as a window, a metaphor, an image to help us conceptualize the love between God and Israel.

As a metaphor, the song is theologically rich. For example, it hints, rather immodestly, that desire is good. Those of us who are tempted to stuff our religious pining down deep—for fear of being disappointed or for fear of seeming out of touch with reality—are hereby freed by a poem like this one to let our longings soar. To be burned up and consumed by our yearning. To see that God himself burns with longing.

Furthermore, the partnership between these two lovers is remarkable. The woman's voice is strong and sure, unembarrassed and unreserved. Clearly, these two are confident, safe, and at peace in one another's arms. Their love allows utter freedom to be themselves, no shame in their bodies, no shame in their desires. Coming together grants them freedom and confidence. The criticism of others rolls off their backs because they each have the unconditional love of the other. When you read between the lines looking for religious implications, once again, the metaphor you find is powerful. Imagine it: we have this level of intimacy with the Divine. We are set free to be that naked—no more fears, no more insecurities, no more doubts. God holds nothing back from us.

Modern biblical scholars, however, are hesitant about jumping to allegorical interpretations and too quickly making this love song about God. After all, God is not actually mentioned. Anyone can see that this is a poem about two very real, very human lovers. An unbiased reader is not likely to see a poem about God. Modern scholarship implores us to let the text be what it is. We might expect the Bible to be PG and family friendly, if not in terms of violence then at least in terms of sex. But we must let the Bible speak for itself. We must let this poem speak for itself rather than impose a sanitized interpretation or twist the meaning to accommodate our moral sensibilities.

It is important to hear—really hear—the erotic, sexual, bodily images of this poem. Because too often the church still tries to separate mind from body, spirit from matter, heaven from earth. But right smack in the center of our holiest book, there appears a tribute to the human body. Material beings, not just spiritual ones, are celebrated. It is an earthy depiction of human love, poetry that depicts love like the unfolding of the spring weather. This song goes against the grain of any religion that attempts to separate the soul from the body in which it resides. It goes against the prudish, anxiety-ridden legalism that requires us to stuff our desires or implies that sex is dirty and unmentionable. And for those reasons and more, the surface meaning of the text—the blatant homage to human sexuality—is important and should not be swept aside.

And yet I do not doubt that this love poem speaks to us of God as well, because love itself speaks to us of God, every time it is invoked. It is not as if we have love for our spouse or a friend or family on one plane and love for God on another plane. We simply have Love. Period. God infuses all our love. God is the energy, the source, the substance of love—at every time and in every place. Everywhere there is love, there is God.

Cynthia Bourgeault says we shouldn't be afraid that love for another human being will divide our heart and distract us from our love for God. She writes, "poets, mystics and lovers have claimed throughout the ages that love does not divide the heart, but is in fact the sole force strong enough to *unite* it."[22] We do have shadow sides to our passions that can stir up division, but Love itself has only the power to unify and purify. Thus we do not love God as one thing among many things, such that saying "yes" to God requires saying "no" to another. "Rather," says Bourgeault, "God is the all-encompassing One who unlocks and sustains my ability to give myself fully to life in all its infinite particularity, including the excruciating particularity of a human beloved."[23]

This, I think, is how the Song of Songs belongs in the biblical canon, with its shameless declaration of unquenchable love. You do not come to understand this book by denying the erotic language, substituting the depth of passion in the poem with pretty little churchy metaphors, safe enough to explain in front of young children. The best you can do is to embrace wholeheartedly the possibility of human love that intense, that special, that exclusively and unwaveringly passionate. You learn such a love only by living it, by striving for it, by believing in it and fighting for it, and by *finding amid the struggle the very energy of God* enlivening your heart and renewing your hope.

I once heard author Brennan Manning tell the story of visiting leprosy colonies, and in one particular colony, he met a woman whose skin was rotted away and whose family had deserted her. After a long life of turmoil and suffering, little education, and nearly no love, she had reached her deathbed. As she was passing from this life to the next, Manning asked her what she saw, and she said this to him, exactly word for word: "The winter is past! The rains are over and gone. Flowers appear on the earth; the season of singing has come, the cooing of doves is heard in our land. The fig tree forms its early fruit; the blossoming vines spread their fragrance. Arise, come, my darling; my beautiful darling, come with me" (Song 2:11-13).

Beloved of God, may your most strenuous struggles eventually lead you straight into the arms of Pure, Encompassing Love. Amen.

Another Way of Seeing

1 Samuel 16:1-13; John 9:1-41
(Covenant Baptist Church)

When Samuel goes to find the next king of Israel, he is explicitly told *not* to pay attention to what the sons of Jesse look like. I find it fascinating that the text first emphasizes how God does not look at the outward appearance, and then when David finally arrives on the scene, the first thing we are told about him is that he is ruddy, with beautiful eyes, and handsome. What is up with that? Are we supposed to ignore outward appearances, or are we supposed to make note of beautiful eyes and handsome features?

If you try to stop noticing the appearance of things, you aren't likely to succeed. If you are human, you cannot deny that beauty is a thing with power, that beauty has a natural pull to it, that without even trying we like beautiful things and beautiful people. But if you are human, then you've also had the experience of suddenly seeing beauty where you had not see it before. In the wrinkles of a person's face, perhaps, in a scorched piece of earth, in a funky piece of art, in a winter-bare tree, in a painful memory, etc. Something you once saw as average, or dismal, or even ugly, you suddenly begin to see in a new light.

I have to wonder: Was David handsome before this moment, or did he walk into this event and suddenly the light of God shone on him or out from him in a whole new way? Or was it not so much David's countenance that changed, but Samuel's vision? In that moment of anointing, did Samuel suddenly see as God sees? Was David's inner radiance miraculously made accessible to Samuel's frail human eyes?

This week I saw the Broadway musical *Wicked*, which tells the story of Elphaba, the Wicked Witch of the West, whose only real wickedness was that, through no fault of her own, she was born with green skin and thus lived her life as a social outcast. At one point she tries to stop her lover from telling her that she is beautiful. "Don't lie to me," she hushes him. He insists, "It's not lying; it's looking at things another way."

So much of spiritual growth is *how* we see what we see. For example, we can look at this church and see a tiny little congregation struggling to make ends meet, which is one type of vision. Or we can look at this church and see a wonderfully intimate family of believers tucked in the woods, listening for God.

I do not mean you should wear rose-colored glasses of denial or that when the going gets tough, you should put on your blinders. Ignoring reality is not spiritual maturity; it is spiritual malpractice. Spiritual vision isn't limited; it is wide, wide, wide. It sees the truth of things, even when truth is painful, but spiritual vision also takes in the silvered hope that lines every despair. Spiritual vision sees resurrection colors budding at the tip of every withered branch. Believers are those who suspect that underneath the sackcloth, the heart of every repenter is gold just waiting to be set free.

The Gospel text today is about Jesus giving sight to a blind man—literal sight to a literally blind man—and I don't want to jump too quickly to spiritual sight and forget that God dealt with physical bodies and physical ailments. Jesus is pretty quick, though, to use this miracle to talk to the Pharisees about their inability to see, and he means this in a spiritual way. I think the spirit and body are connected here: that even when we are talking about spiritual sight, there is a physical component to it. What you *actually see* when you look out your window into the backyard has a spiritual nuance. Do you look outside and see the long list of projects you've got to complete? Look out and see the grass that already needs mowing? Or do you look out and see the miracle of a budding plant or the gorgeous perch of a bird on a tree branch? Do you not really see anything at all but give your yard a blank stare while focusing your attention on your worries and fears? What do you see?

In her poem, "A Valentine for Ernest Mann," Naomi Shihab Nye writes,

Once I knew a man who gave his wife
two skunks for a valentine.
He couldn't understand why she was crying.
"I thought they had such beautiful eyes."
And he was serious. He was a serious man
who lived in a serious way. Nothing was ugly
just because the world said so. He really
liked those skunks. So, he reinvented them
as valentines and they became beautiful.
At least, to him. And the poems that had been hiding
in the eyes of the skunks for centuries
crawled out and curled up at his feet.

Maybe if we reinvent whatever our lives give us
we find poems. Check your garage, the odd sock
in your drawer, the person you almost like, but not quite.
And let me know.[24]

What do you see? Is it made handsome by the light and anointing of God, or are you so absorbed in the superficial that the deeper beauty of a thing is not readily visible to you? What you see with your physical eyes tells you something about the state of your soul. When you look into the eyes of your neighbor, do you see her worth looking back at you? Can you find in the features of any face the markings of God's imprint?

Beauty is in the eye of the beholder, they say, and the important thing here is that the beholder is you. Your eyes will discover beauty where your eyes look for beauty. I wonder if the saints look out into the world and the sea of humanity and only see beauty.

Of course, Samuel does pick only one king, so there is not just new vision happening here, but also discernment. It is unlikely that you and I are going to be choosing the next king anytime soon, but we do make lots of decisions every day from a long lineup of potential choices. How do we know what to choose in life? What career, what new endeavor, what charity, what ways of spending our time and resources and energy? Lately I have been practicing discernment by looking for the choice that glitters at me. I do not mean the glamorous option, the sequins-covered option, the flashy, everyone-thinks-it-is-fabulous option. That would be to look at outward appearances only with spiritually impoverished sight. I mean I choose the option God seems to be shining on or shining out from in that moment for me. If I squint my soul's eyes just right, I catch a gleam in one thing or another. Some little shimmer that says to my soul, "Pick me." This isn't a foolproof way to make decisions, but it sure beats making a pros and cons list. It has definitely taught me a thing or two about trust and risk, and it constantly lands me in the dazzling presence of the unexpected.

What in your life is asking to be anointed? Maybe there is something you are being called to, and you've shoved it over to the side like the runt of the litter, but God is telling you, "Go ahead and bless that. Go ahead and take your passion off the back burner and bring it to the front. Stop simmering. Let yourself boil. See beauty and potential where no one else has seen it before, and then you will have found your purpose."

Also, *who* is your life needs anointing? Who have you previously passed over as undeserving of God's favor? If you looked closer, God would tell you, "I love that one so much." Get out your anointing oil and slather it all over the kid picked last in the lineup for football, and see if he starts to glisten in a whole new way. If that kid was you, slather yourself.

What I am saying is, take oil with you everywhere. Help make as many things shiny as you possibly can. If you stop and pause and anoint the things of this earth, other people will pause too, and it will be like washing mud from their eyes. They will see what you see, if you show them. And they will help you see what they see, if only you ask, "What do you find beautiful?"

In high school, I read this story in Brennan Manning's *The Ragamuffin Gospel*, and it has stuck with me ever since:

> In his book *Mortal Lessons*, Richard Selzer, M.D., writes, "I stand by the bed where a young woman lies, her face postoperative, her mouth twisted in palsy, clownish. A tiny twig of the facial nerve, the one to the muscles of her mouth, has been severed. She will be thus from now on. The surgeon had followed with religious fervor the curve of her flesh; I promise you that. Nevertheless, to remove the tumor in her cheek, I had to cut the little nerve.

Her young husband is in the room. He stands on the opposite side of the bed and together they seem to dwell in the evening lamplight, isolated from me, private. Who are they, I ask myself, he and this wry mouth I have made, who gaze at and touch each other so generously, greedily? The young woman speaks.

'Will my mouth always be like this?' she asks.

'Yes,' I say, 'it will. It is because the nerve was cut.'

She nods and is silent. But the young man smiles.

'I like it,' he says. 'It is kind of cute.'

All at once I know who he is. I understand and I lower my gaze. One is not bold in an encounter with a god. Unmindful, he bends to kiss her crooked mouth and I am so close I can see how he twists his own lips to accommodate hers, to show her that their kiss still works."[25]

May we be given God-eyes and restored vision so that everywhere we look, we see the things God sees, the way God sees them, like looking at a painting through the eyes of its artist. May we come to appreciate every hue and shade; may we drench the world in oil. Amen.

legs:
authority in preaching

Of all the themes I could write on, this is the least expected. I do not like authority or the word *a-u-t-h-o-r-i-t-y*, but if you take off *i-t-y*, you are left with *author*, and suddenly I am in the word I thought I hated.

Authority makes me think of uncaring, unbending rules. It brings to mind a small group of old white men who know neither me nor reality and yet make up lines the rest of us are not allowed to cross. It makes me think of dominance and control. It makes me think of one person having say-so over another person.

It also makes me think of the dreaded word *submission.* When I was a married pastor, people who were perplexed by me occasionally asked, "How does being a pastor work with marriage? How do you submit to your husband? Does he have to submit to you as his pastor?" It was a hierarchy contradiction that some folks just couldn't wrap their minds around.

I didn't quite know how to answer, because to explain, "I don't submit to anyone, thank you very much, but also, no one is expected to submit to me," sounded too explosive to say out loud. This is why women as preachers are so hard to swallow: the unhealthy fanatical deference given to the title *pastor* is hard to maintain when the title belongs to a woman. It is confusing and disorienting to people when the seed of Eve takes the pulpit. It topples everything.

Wonderfully, beautifully, thankfully, it topples everything.

I have long despised the word *leader. I am not a leader and I am not an authority figure*—that's what I would tell you if you asked. Most assuredly, you do *not* have to do what I say. As a spiritual guide, I want to free you, not confine you, send you light and love and grace, not mandates and guilt and tasks. I want to respect you as an intelligent, passionate person in your own right, capable of living well without my help and input. Just as I have longed to be respected in that way myself, I now offer such respect as gift to you.

How do my instincts and impulses about how to treat people relate to typical understandings of leadership and authority? For a long time I was convinced that my instincts to honor the other and refrain from giving advice ran counter to the idea of leadership.

Then I read Brené Brown's definition of a leader: "anyone who holds her- or himself accountable for finding potential in people and processes,"[26] and I thought, *Well, okay, I could almost get behind that, but do we have to call it* leadership? Then I read Henri Nouwen's description of leadership as the articulation of the inner life. He wrote, "The Christian leader is, therefore, first of all, a man who is willing to put his own articulated faith at the disposal of those who ask his help . . . ,"[27] and I thought, *Goodness, that is exactly what I attempt to do: articulate the inner life.* And then I read what Dawna Markova says about authority being authorship, the "authoring of our own existence," or "to be in a life of our own definition." She points out that *author, authentic, authenticity,* and *authoritative* all have the same root, meaning genuine.[28] I read this, and suddenly the whole world shifted.

I realized that authority and leadership have nothing to do with who follows you and everything to do with inner authority and outward authenticity. You aren't trying to lead anyone. You are striving to live out of your deepest center, and inevitably (but apart from any attempt on your part to make this happen) people will begin to listen to you because we all crave being around people who live authentically. People may follow you, but you certainly aren't *trying* to take them anywhere. You are listening to what speaks to you, and then you are finding the wits and stamina and courage to use your legs and follow the inner voice. So few people walk this path that if you walk it, it will seem remarkable to folks, but you aren't being remarkable. You are just living. Finally, really living.

If you spend your energy figuring out what other people need to do and fretting about how to get them there, you will end up frustrated, disappointed, and utterly burnt out. If you spend all your energy finding what you are meant to do (and then doing it), you will be formidable and fierce and free in the best sense.

When my little church experienced one of its first crises, I got to work immediately, doing what needed to be done. I had no idea what to do, really, but I just did the next right thing, one day at a time. I was shocked when church members began to tell me, "I appreciate the way you've led our church during this time."

Is that what I was doing? Leading? I had no idea. I thought I was just doing the needed thing. I wasn't trying to motivate anyone or make anything happen. I was merely organizing the chaos so we could all get a bit of a handle on what to do next, if possible. But people perceived it as leadership, and that intrigued me.

Maybe leadership is what happens when you least expect it. If you want to be a leader, don't take a class on it or read a book or attend a seminar. Just get somewhere quiet and ask yourself the primal question, "Where do I want to go, even if no one follows me?" Answer the question eventually, even if the answer scares you. Then go there. Even if no one follows. Go there. Then you will have found your authenticity. You will have found the authorship of your own life. You will have found authority.

Authority has nothing to do with dominance. It cares not who follows. It is not competitive or manipulative or controlling. It is free-spirited and wild. It is strong and it is undaunted. It is powerful and it is gentle. It is dynamic and vibrant and magnetic. It is energy. It is force but not coercion. It has earthquake potential, but it builds no thrones. It is life-force, love-force, growth-force. Authority, authorship, authenticity is telling the story the way you choose to tell it, and the way you tell a story can change everything.

But every good story must ring true. It will not be an authentic rendering if you lie, twist reality, or hide your truest self. Storytelling is the gateway into shaping life and community, but to be a good storyteller, you must be a truthful one.

This brings me back to the word *submission*, which turns out not to be so taboo in my life after all. I do a lot of submitting, in fact. I submit (as best I can) to what is being asked of me in the moment. I do not mean the demands and expectations and drives that generally yank us hither and thither and never let us touch our center. I mean submitting to what is necessary, what is calling me forward, no matter how small or how strange or how difficult it may seem.

I also submit to the truth of things, to reality as best I can. It is amazing what lengths humans will go to avoid reality and the truth of what is happening in front of their eyes because it is too painful, disorienting, uncomfortable, unexpected, or beyond one's control. So I try to stay awake to what is real. To sleepwalk, to remain comatose, to grip and to control: all of this is resistance to your best work and is failure to submit to real living. Ironically, the people most awake get labeled rebels because their surrender to Life is so unusual it appears radical.

And finally I submit one to another, just as the Bible suggests. At least, I try to, and here is what I think it means: Submit and allow people to be who they are, move at their pace, think their own thoughts, and feel their own feelings. Respect their conscience and their decisions just as I want my conscience and my decisions respected. Submit to the mystery of humanity—that we are all so different and yet so much the same. Live bold and wild and free, but never trample on the heads of others to get there. Submit to compassion by never being violent, coercive, or mean. Accept that others' choices will not always make sense to me, but that does not mean they aren't the beloved of God. When other people act unjustly or violently or unkindly, I *can* stand up to that and I *can* set boundaries. It is never the case that I must submit to the oppression of self or others. But I can submit to the beauty I see in you while still honoring the beauty in me.

Will You Sing for My Daughter?

Judges 11:30-40 (Baptist University of the Americas, San Antonio, Texas)

She stands in the frame of the front door, hands trembling, legs shaking. She grabs the wall to steady herself. She stands there dried-eyed and pain-stricken, frozen to the spot, paralyzed . . . .

She is watching the back of her daughter walk away from her, those slender legs taking her slowly up the side of the hill.

It's a familiar sight, and temporarily her mind is carried away to other times. She remembers those same legs, only shorter and a little stubbier, running up the hill, zigzagging and laughing, curls blowing in the wind.

The mother almost loses herself to the memory, but the horror of the present returns unrelenting, creeping up her spine like ice, and when it reaches her throat, for a minute she cannot breathe.

The memory fades and her eyes refocus on the scene in front of her—the same hill, the same daughter, the same green grass and small struggling trees as before, but the one new element is the makeshift table-like structure sitting on the top of the hill.

She had peeked in on her husband building it late into the night. He was sweating from the labor and crying from the burden, and she caught a glimpse of a man wrestling and confused. She will never forgive him, but she did pity him that night. Seeing those tears roll down his cheek was the first time she had felt compassion for him in two months.

The first month had been filled with screeching and begging and wailing, but he would not listen to her. "I made a vow!" he boomed. "I am a man of my word. Do not question me, Woman."

The second month had been filled with absolute silence. They had not spoken to each other one time. At night she slept as far away from his side of the bed as possible. They kept their backs to each other, and as she laid in the darkness, she tried to pretend she was really alone.

After all, that's what she was, wasn't she? Alone.

What good is a man in your bed without a man by your side? They may have only been inches away in the sheets, but they were miles apart in their hearts. It had become an irredeemable chasm between them.

Two months had passed far too fast, and now The Day is here. As she watches her daughter walk the hill towards the altar, she remembers a story her own father used to tell her—the story about Abraham and his son Isaac and how God had provided a ram to save Isaac. She breathes to the heavens, "Could you send a ram? I'm begging you. That's my daughter. Please."

By the time the prayer finishes choking its way out of her constricted throat, her daughter has dutifully reached the top of the hill, and the mother shuts her eyes. There is a long pause. She hears a scream and squeezes her eyes tighter. She begins shaking, and she doesn't remember falling to the ground, but that's where her husband finds her when he returns, curled on the ground moaning. He grabs her by the arms and holds her tight. She opens her eyes, but when she sees the blood smear on his face, she closes them again and convulses.

"Was there a ram?" she murmurs.

Silence.

"*Was there a ram?*" Now she is screaming.

He squeezes her arms even tighter. "I . . . don't . . . understand," he chokes out in a whisper.

"Damn you, Jephthah, tell me. Tell me if there was a ram. Like the ram for Isaac. Was there a ram for *her?*"

There are tears streaming down his lined face. "There was no ram," he whispers with regret. He is looking into the desperate face of his wife, but suddenly he is seeing a hundred women's faces, all the mothers whose sons he's killed in war, and he knows there is too much blood on his hands to ever know peace again, but he says none of this out loud. He only tries to hold her close, but she reacts violently, shoves him with force. "Don't touch me," she says and she walks away.

In the weeks and months that follow, Jephthah the war hero wanders through town in a daze. The people thank him, congratulate him for his valiant efforts on the battlefield, to which he shakes his head and grunts.

The priest comes by their house to express his sorrow for their loss of a daughter but also to praise Jephthah for his unwavering devotion to the Lord. Jephthah's wife will not even acknowledge the priest's presence or serve him food. Jephthah uncomfortably shakes the priest's hand, thanks him for coming. His wife grabs a pot of boiling water and hurls it at them both, but the pot is heavy and her aim is wild and it misses them and smashes into the wall. The priest forgives her on account of her grief, and the whole city comes to know the wife of Jephthah as the one who lost her mind and tried to scald a priest.

She cares not what they think. Every day she walks to the top of the grassy hill, muttering to herself. At the top of the hill she sits, and then she sings. Softly at first, like a whisper only she can hear, but eventually her daughter's friends join her. These are the dear ones who'd spent two months wailing together with their friend, and now they circle around the mother and listen close to hear her song. "What can we do for you?" they ask with broken hearts.

"Sing with me," she says.

Will you sing for my daughter,
will you sing for her soul?
For the life taken from her,
before she grew old?
Will you sing for my daughter,
will you sing for her soul?
For the life taken from her,
before she grew old?

"Yes. Yes."

We will sing for your daughter,
we will sing for her soul,
for the life taken from her,
before she grew old.

And so they do. They sing and they sing and they sing until their voices rise throughout the land. They sing through the gathering dark of dusk, they sing through the long dark night, they sing through the coming of sunrise and the heat of the noonday. On the third day, there is no resurrection, and so on they sing. At the end of the fourth day they decide together, *We will do this every year, for four days each time. Every year until we are gone, we will gather and we will tell the tale of Jephthah's daughter, and she will never be forgotten. And when the companions grow old and their voices grow dim, their daughters take up the task, and then their daughters, and then their daughters . . . .*

And one day, many generations later, there was a prophet to God's people, named Isaiah, whose mother used to sing to him when he was a child:

We will sing for your daughter,
we will sing for her soul,
for the life taken from her,
before she grew old.

And with this melody in his heart he wrote these words:

Such fasting as you do today
will not make your voice heard on high.
Is this the fast that I choose?
A day to humble oneself?
To bow down the head like a bulrush?
To lie down in sackcloth and ashes?
Will you call this a fast,
a day acceptable to the Lord?
Is not this the fast that I choose:
to loose the bonds of injustice,
to undo the thongs of the yoke,

to let the oppressed go free
and to break every yoke? (Isa 58:4b-6)

And centuries after that there was a man named Jesus, and one day he meandered to the top of a grassy hill where his followers gathered around him, and over the chatter and clamor of the crowds, a tune played in his head. Because he was Jewish, he knew all the stories of the Bible, and because he was God, he heard all the songs of bloodshed the earth had been singing since the beginning of violent men, since the ground first cried out to God from swallowing Abel's blood. And with songs of the ages echoing in his head, he said to the people:

Blessed are those that mourn,
for they shall be comforted. (Matt 5:4)

And later, as he hung on a cross, the wife of Jephthah grabbed the hand of God the Father, and together they looked away, for it is unbearable to watch your child die. "I will sing for your son," she whispered, and all the angels of heaven nodded their heads in agreement.

And sometime after that, the Apostle John, on the Island of Patmos, was humming to himself a tune from his mother's bosom (*"will you sing for my daughter . . ."*) when he had a vision from on high, and he wrote the words,

Worthy, worthy, worthy
is the Lamb who was slain. (Rev 5:12)

My friends, in a violent world of passionate but confused religion, may we never build altars on which we sacrifice people in the name of our ideals. May we always and forever be the ones who sing on behalf of the slain, and, where possible, may we stop the axe before it reaches the innocent. May we preach not the God of war but the God of the cross, who joined the suffering ones and wept. Amen.

Wannabe Pacifists

Matthew 5:38-48 (Covenant Baptist Church)

At one of our retreats here at Covenant, we gathered around in a circle and sort of pretended to be Quakers, the way we sort of pretend to be Franciscans at some of our other retreats. In this instance, we were gathering for a full hour of silence, which is the way Quakers gather every week. Before we began, Gordon and Jeanene explained the way it was going to work. How you were only to speak if the Spirit of God prompted you to speak. How you should not go into the hour thinking you would speak, nor should you go into it thinking you would not speak. You entered it wide open, no preset predictions. When someone else spoke, you listened. You did not interrupt; you did not react. You only listened. You did not look directly at the person who was speaking. You looked elsewhere as a symbol of the fact that you believed the words they were speaking came from Elsewhere, from Spirit, from On High.

I spend a lot of time in silence by myself, but I anxiously wondered if it would feel strange, if it would feel like forever, to be so quiet with a group of people. It ended up being a profound experience for me. That was about a year and a half ago, I believe. I can still tell you which handful of people spoke for a minute into the silence, and in some cases I could even tell you what was said.

I did not speak, but I did have a couple of thoughts that came to me unbidden during that time.

One thought was this: *Wow, if I were Quaker, Sunday mornings would be so much easier. No planning, no preaching. I wonder if I can talk the church into becoming Quaker.*

But the second thought, which took me by surprise, came to me clear as day: *Only a Quaker could become a pacifist.*

I knew that this statement didn't actually mean Quakers are the only people in the world who are pacifists. But sitting there Quaker-style, receiving openly in silence whatever people offered, made me realize that only someone who practices acceptance and open reception with intentionality and regularity could ever grow a pacifist heart.

Conceptually, I've long been a wannabe pacifist. My heart wishes pacifism was the answer, but my head can always come up with an exception where an act of violence seems called for. I think we would all agree that we live in a world with way too much violence. But nearly all of us could think of at least one example where a violent act could be an appropriate response or a necessary evil in preventing further violence: stopping Hitler, for example, or protecting a child whose safety is being threatened.

But I'm not so sure anymore that pacifism is about the rationale for what we would do in a hypothetical situation so much as it is a condition of the heart to which we aspire. I recently read where Parker Palmer described himself as a would-be pacifist, and I thought, *yes, me too!* (And wouldn't you know, Parker Palmer is a Quaker?) It seems that pacifism, or the capacity to respond nonviolently, is less of an intellectual position than it is a state of being to which one aspires but likely fails. It isn't a stance you take or don't take in your mind, weighing it rationally against "the just war" theory or other theories.

For one thing, Jesus' choices weren't always rational, were they? He chose children and lepers and outcasts for companions; he picked a cross over a throne. It wasn't the best logic, but it was the best of love the world has ever known.

Pacifism is a startling, God-given aptitude for kindness in the face of horror—an aptitude one can only grow over the course of a lifetime. It is creativity in response to desperate times that only something Holy can evoke.

Jesus says love your enemies and turn the other cheek, and if someone sues you for your shirt, give them your coat too, and I don't think this is mere hyperbole. I think it's gospel truth, but truth that comes in the form of a pill too big to swallow the first time around. It is not the sort of thing a spoon full of sugar will help go down. It is something that gets down past your defenses one little jolt at a time, like a long elevator ride that stops at every floor, letting more bitterness out, letting more messengers of mercy in. This is not the kind of thing you can explain in an essay. It is the kind of advice you only begin to unwrap as you live a life of radical grace-giving.

With that being said, consider this: I care deeply about battered women and children, and I know you care too, so I think that whatever interpretation of a Scripture we arrive at, it has to be something we could say to a battered woman. Whatever definition you give to "turn the other cheek," could you say it to a child with a bruised eye or a woman with a broken arm?

I am not talking about twisting Scripture to make it accommodate our sensibilities. I am saying that looking in the eye of an oppressed person when you read the Bible is a good, solid exegetical tool that is as Jesus-y as interpretation gets. Jesus was always putting people ahead of the rules, ahead of the Sabbath, ahead of religious taboos. Healing and deliverance were his trump cards; love over law, every time.

So as we engage the painstaking, lifelong task of interpreting Scripture and following Jesus, we keep the suffering children in our hearts and know that discernment is required. That allowing the innocent to be slaughtered isn't what pacifism or Jesus is about. Rather, we ask ourselves, what in our lives deserves protecting? Is there a nonviolent way to protect it? Can I keep love in my heart even towards those I must stand against? None of the questions gets answered easily, but asking them is the first step.

And finally, it is often said that we are our own worst enemies. We are always sabotaging ourselves, inhibiting our best work, blocking our joy, holding back our vibrancy, either from laziness or selfishness or poor stewardship of our time. What would it mean to love the enemy inside you? Instead of shaming yourself for what you do not like about you, what if you took a long, compassionate look at all your grotesque parts and whispered gently over them, "I love you. I see you. I hear you. We're going to figure this out together, okay?" Maybe there is so much war in the world because we are all at war in our souls. Maybe pacifism is first and foremost an inside job. Maybe we first begin to learn peacemaking in solitude. Maybe the contemplative journey of harmonizing the inner life is where we start the outward journey towards a peaceful earth. Maybe befriending what we used to be ashamed of in here is the gateway to relating better to the strangers we meet out there. Instead of shouting at your insecurities and fears to go away, try holding hands with them, and see if they grow friendlier towards you. Wouldn't it be simpler to love your neighbor if there were less hostility and competition waging war within your own person?

I don't know about you, but if I close my eyes, I can picture the faces of people I know who are a challenge to my capacity for mercy. There are a few people in my life that I don't know how to love, and I can tell you I'm not going to have it figured out by tomorrow, and certainly not by the end of this sermon. But I can also tell you that I'm going to walk down the path of love and not the path of hate. If it takes me my whole life and then some to figure out how to love the people who wound me, then I guess we know one of the ways I'll be spending a life: learning how to love.

One of the things I've learned so far is that you don't have to let people hurt you; sometimes love is tough and sometimes love says no. Turning the other cheek doesn't mean you take abuse; it means you don't hit back. The typical reaction is to take an eye for an eye, but the Jesus way is not to retaliate. The typical reaction is to demonize the one who struck you; the Jesus way is to turn your head and look them in the eye and remember they are human. It gets a little confusing to watch Jesus die, because sometimes it seems like we are meant to be martyrs, allowing ourselves be slaughtered and our best selves to be sabotaged. But we must remember the resurrection. Jesus didn't stay dead. The Christian message isn't one of defeat or death or doormats. The Christian message is one of victory, life, and power, though you come to it in counterintuitive ways, through grace and mercy, acceptance and rest, rather than battle and competition, striving and perfection. Jesus did not, for so much as a second, give up in the face of evil; he was only ever giving in to the power of love.

I think, for the most part, the church is a group of wannabe pacifists who still spend their days swinging their fists at their enemies, at their neighbors, and at their own imperfections. For you and me, peace is still just a tiny seed we've planted and continue to water. The hour of worship is where we come to look for its budding and fertilize its soil. I can't imagine how I'm ever going to look anything like Jesus, but sometimes when I am here, I watch your kindness and am reminded that, by golly, we are on our way to holiness after all.

May we dare to try it: loving our enemies, praying for those who persecute us, going the second mile. May we be about *these* wild and radical Jesusy things: The refusal to retaliate. The gumption to look a madman in the eye and search for the remnant of his soul. The audacity to be generous. The courage to let our fear of the other drain away. The capacity to get creative instead of mean when things get ugly. The miracle of holding hands with people whom we have a hard time believing belong in our circle.

As for embodying the radical, unrealistic, but made-real-in-Jesus-Christ love of God: I don't think we are ever going to get there, ever going to replicate it with precision, but we are going to forge a way towards it, and we are going to make many friends along the way, and we are going to die grateful that we brushed up against a thing so beautiful as love even in this war-torn lifetime. Amen.

epilogue

pReachıng, at ıts Best, is a full-body experience. It engages the whole of who you are—mind, body, spirit—in the same way that faith, hope, and love are supposed to captivate you from the core of your soul to the tips of your toes. Proclaiming is Word enacted, and such an act exercises your whole being. If you do it right, nothing gets left out or shut out.

The way I see it, there is a fleshy muscle to preaching that has nothing to do with brute coercion and everything to do with inner strength and quiet power. There are long fingers to preaching that hold hands with the hurting, caress the unlovely, tap the shoulders of the distracted, reach into the hearts of listeners and stir the pots where we all keep things brewing. There are eyes to preaching that see the world a tad askew and full of vibrant color. There are knees to preaching that know when to kneel and ask and when to stand tall and speak. There are ears to preaching, collecting sounds and silences, the wisdom of the ages, and the prayers of the people with long patience and unflinching reverence. There are toes to preaching for dipping into unfamiliar waters and testing the flow, unlocking the necessary practice of curiosity for all who want to wade the river beneath the river. There is a womb to preaching where seeds go to grow. There is a nervous system to preaching, placing feelers out into the world, collecting data via sensation, perceiving pain and pleasure, interpreting experience, and finally giving it words.

This is preaching: to live and breathe holy words. Inhale spirit. Exhale power. Inhale story. Exhale truth. Inhale. Exhale. In. Out. Never stop breathing in. When your lungs are full, never hold your breath. Amen.

Notes

1. *Ruah* is Hebrew for wind, breath, spirit.

2. Eugene Peterson, *The Contemplative Pastor* (Grand Rapids MI: Eerdman's, 1989) 18.

3. Clarissa Pinkola Estés, *Women Who Run With the Wolves* (New York: Ballantine Books, 1992) 432.

4. Dawna Markova, *I Will Not Die an Unlived Life: Reclaiming Purpose and Passion* (Berkeley CA: Conari, 2000) 68.

5. My paraphrase of Genesis 4:10, though I followed pretty closely to the text.

6. Habakkuk 2:9-11.

7. Luke 19:47.

8. 2 Corinthians 4:10.

9. Frederick Buechner, *Listening to Your Life* (San Francisco: HarperSanFrancisco, 1992) 206.

10. Father Gregory Boyle, "Fr. Greg Boyle—The Calling of Delight: Gangs, Service, and Kinship," *On Being*, interview with Krista Tippett, 26 February 2013, http://www.onbeing.org/program/father-greg-boyle-on-the-calling-of-delight/5053 (accessed 19 June 2014).

11. Rumi, "Spring Giddiness," trans. Coleman Barks, *The Essential Rumi: New Expanded Edition* (New York: HarperOne, 2004) 36.

12. Rumi, "Today Like Every Other Day," trans. Coleman Barks, *Risking Everything: 110 Poems of Love and Revelation* (New York: Harmony, 2003).

13. Richard Rohr, *Everything Belongs: The Gift of Contemplative Prayer*, updated and rev. ed. (New York: Crossroad Publishing, 2003) 98.

14. Eugene Peterson, *A Long Obedience in the Same Direction: Discipleship in an Instant Society* (Downers Grove IL: InterVarsity Press, 2000).

15. Henri J. M. Nouwen, *The Wounded Healer: Ministry in Contemporary Society* (New York: Doubleday, 1972) 39.

16. Clarissa Pinkola Estés, *Women Who Run with the Wolves* (New York: Ballantine: 1992) 25–26.

17. Jan Frazier, *Words to Wake Up To,* CD, written and read by Jan Frazier, copyright 2008.

18. Brené Brown, *Daring Greatly: How the Courage to Be Vulnerable Transforms the Way We Live, Love, Parent, and Lead* (New York: Gotham Books, 2012).

19. Richard Rohr, *Everything Belongs,* 25.

20. Scott Cairns, "Adventures in New Testament Greek: Metanoia," *Compass of Affection: Poems New and Selected* (Brewster MA: Paraclete Press, 2006) 93.

21. Rumi, "The Guest House," trans. Coleman Barks.

22. Cynthia Bourgeault, *The Meaning of Mary Magdalene: Discovering the Woman at the Heart of Christianity* (Boston: Shambala, 2010) 92.

23. Ibid., 91.

24. Naomi Shihab Nye, "A Valentine for Ernest Mann," *Red Suitcase* (Rochester NY: BOA Editions, Ltd., 1994) 70.

25. Richard Selzer, quoted by Brennan Manning in *The Ragamuffin Gospel,* (Portland OR: Multnomah, 1990) 104–105.

26. Brown, *Daring Greatly,* 185.

27. Nouwen, *Wounded Healer,* 38.

28. Markova, *I Will Not Die an Unlived Life,* 125.

Acknowledgments

First I need to thank Aurelia. Without your unfaltering belief in me, I may never have made it through 2013, much less written a whole book.

Thank you to Paul Soupiset—you not only did an amazing job designing the cover, you also encouraged my writing in huge ways, as well as read the entire manuscript thoroughly, offering useful edits and remarks. I am so grateful!

Thank you, Covenant Baptist Church, my dearly beloved congregation, without whom I would not have these stories to tell nor these sermons to share. You are a remarkably generous people who have allowed me to blossom in safety with your patience, wisdom, and support. You inspire me.

Thank you to my family, for supporting me through my life's most difficult season, for standing by me, believing me, and showing up when I needed it most.

Thank you to Burt Burleson for teaching me how to pastor, and for awakening me to the notion that my love of words had a place in the hour of worship.

Thank you to Pam Durso, for believing I should write a book and for helping me get there.

Thank you to Carla and Viva! Books for inspiring my words and offering a haven for local artists and emerging mystics.

Thank you to Austin Poetry Slam and the San Antonio Sun Poets Society for helping me find my voice! Your enthusiastic embrace of my craft was a turning point in my confidence.

Thank you to the wonderful professors who have shaped me into the person I am today. Both Southern Nazarene University and Truett Seminary have shaped my journey and supported me on the path to being one of the few (but growing number!) of female Baptist pastors. Thank you to Dr. Green, Dr. Crutcher, Dr.

Michelson, Dr. Tucker, Dr. Gloer, Dr. Sands, and all of you who sharpened my thinking and promoted my growth.

Thank you, D., Tina, Catherine, Kathleen, Marjorie for showing me what empowered women look like, and for embracing me into the circle of strong and intuitive women. Thank you to my Merton reading group for providing a quiet space just to be.

Thank you to Megan Chaffin for designing my website and doing a beautiful job.

Thank you, Smyth & Helwys Publishing, for taking my dream of a book and turning it into a printed reality!

Thank you to my readers, for without you, writing would be of little consequence. May we continue to inspire one another towards a kinder, more compassionate world for many years to come.

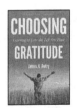

Contextualizing the Gospel
A Homiletic Commentary on 1 Corinthians

Brian L. Harbour

Harbour examines every part of Paul's letter, providing a rich resource for those who want to struggle with the difficult texts as well as the simple texts, who want to know how God's word—all of it—intersects with their lives today. *978-1-57312-589-5 240 pages/pb* **$19.00**

Dance Lessons
Moving to the Beat of God's Heart

Jeanie Miley

Miley shares her joys and struggles a she learns to "dance" with the Spirit of the Living God. *978-1-57312-622-9 240 pages/pb* **$19.00**

A Divine Duet
Ministry and Motherhood

Alicia Davis Porterfield, ed.

Each essay in this inspiring collection is as different as the mother-minister who wrote it, from theologians to chaplains, inner-city ministers to rural-poverty ministers, youth pastors to preachers, mothers who have adopted, birthed, and done both.

978-1-57312-676-2 146 pages/pb **$16.00**

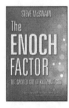

The Enoch Factor
The Sacred Art of Knowing God

Steve McSwain

The Enoch Factor is a persuasive argument for a more enlightened religious dialogue in America, one that affirms the goals of all religions—guiding followers in self-awareness, finding serenity and happiness, and discovering what the author describes as "the sacred art of knowing God." *978-1-57312-556-7 256 pages/pb* **$21.00**

Ethics as if Jesus Mattered
Essays in Honor of Glen H. Stassen

Rick Axtell, Michelle Tooley, Michael L. Westmoreland-White, eds.

Ethics as if Jesus Mattered will introduce Stassen's work to a new generation, advance dialogue and debate in Christian ethics, and inspire more faithful discipleship just as it honors one whom the contributors consider a mentor. *978-1-57312-695-3 234 pages/pb* **$18.00**

Healing Our Hurts
Coping with Difficult Emotions
Daniel Bagby

In *Healing Our Hurts*, Daniel Bagby identifies and explains all the dynamics at play in these complex emotions. Offering practical biblical insights to these feelings, he interprets faith-based responses to separate overly religious piety from true, natural human emotion. This book helps us learn how to deal with life's difficult emotions in a redemptive and responsible way. *978-1-57312-613-7 144 pages/pb $15.00*

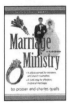

Marriage Ministry: A Guidebook
Bo Prosser and Charles Qualls

This book is equally helpful for ministers, for nearly/newlywed couples, and for thousands of couples across our land looking for fresh air in their marriages. *1-57312-432-X 160 pages/pb $16.00*

Hope for the Thinking Christian
Seeking a Path of Faith through Everyday Life
Stephen Reese

Readers who want to confront their faith more directly, to think it through and be open to God in an individual, authentic, spiritual encounter will find a resonant voice in Stephen Reese.

978-1-57312-553-6 160 pages/pb $16.00

A Hungry Soul Desperate to Taste God's Grace
Honest Prayers for Life
Charles Qualls

Part of how we *see* God is determined by how we *listen* to God. There is so much noise and movement in the world that competes with images of God. This noise would drown out God's beckoning voice and distract us. Charles Qualls's newest book offers readers prayers for that journey toward the meaning and mystery of God. *978-1-57312-648-9 152 pages/pb $14.00*

I'm Trying to Lead... Is Anybody Following?
The Challenge of Congregational Leadership in the Postmodern World
Charles B. Bugg

Bugg provides us with a view of leadership that has theological integrity, honors the diversity of church members, and reinforces the brave hearts of church leaders who offer vision and take risks in the service of Christ and the church. *978-1-57312-731-8 136 pages/pb $13.00*

To order call **1-800-747-3016** or visit **www.helwys.com**

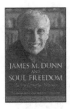

James M. Dunn and Soul Freedom
Aaron Douglas Weaver

James Milton Dunn, over the last fifty years, has been the most aggressive Baptist proponent for religious liberty in the United States. Soul freedom—voluntary, uncoerced faith and an unfettered individual conscience before God—is the basis of his understanding of church-state separation and the historic Baptist basis of religious liberty. *978-1-57312-590-1 224 pages/pb* **$18.00**

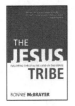

The Jesus Tribe
Following Christ in the Land of the Empire
Ronnie McBrayer

The Jesus Tribe fleshes out the implications, possibilities, contradictions, and complexities of what it means to live within the Jesus Tribe and in the shadow of the American Empire.

978-1-57312-592-5 208 pages/pb **$17.00**

Judaism
A Brief Guide to Faith and Practice
Sharon Pace

Sharon Pace's newest book is a sensitive and comprehensive introduction to Judaism. What is it like to be born into the Jewish community? How does belief in the One God and a universal morality shape the way in which Jews see the world? How does one find meaning in life and the courage to endure suffering? How does one mark joy and forge community ties? *978-1-57312-644-1 144 pages/pb* **$16.00**

Let Me More of Their Beauty See
Reading Familiar Verses in Context
Diane G. Chen

Let Me More of Their Beauty See offers eight examples of how attention to the historical and literary settings can safeguard against taking a text out of context, bring out its transforming power in greater dimension, and help us apply Scripture appropriately in our daily lives.

978-1-57312-564-2 160 pages/pb **$17.00**

Living Call
An Old Church and a Young Minister Find Life Together
Tony Lankford

This light look at church and ministry highlights the dire need for fidelity to the vocation of church leadership. It also illustrates Lankford's conviction that the historic, local congregation has a beautiful, vibrant, and hopeful future. *978-1-57312-702-8 112 pages/pb* **$12.00**

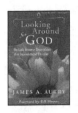

Looking Around for God
The Strangely Reverent Observations of an Unconventional Christian
James A. Autry

Looking Around for God, Autry's tenth book, is in many ways his most personal. In it he considers his unique life of faith and belief in God. Autry is a former Fortune 500 executive, author, poet, and consultant whose work has had a significant influence on leadership thinking.

978-157312-484-3 *144 pages/pb* **$16.00**

Making the Timeless Word Timely
A Primer for Preachers
Michael B. Brown

Michael Brown writes, "There is a simple formula for sermon preparation that creates messages that apply and engage whether your parish is rural or urban, young or old, rich or poor, five thousand members or fifty." The other part of the task, of course, involves being creative and insightful enough to know how to take the general formula for sermon preparation and make it particular in its impact on a specific congregation. Brown guides the reader through the formula and the skills to employ it with excellence and integrity.

978-1-57312-578-9 *160 pages/pb* **$16.00**

Meeting Jesus Today
For the Cautious, the Curious, and the Committed
Jeanie Miley

Meeting Jesus Today, ideal for both individual study and small groups, is intended to be used as a workbook. It is designed to move readers from studying the Scriptures and ideas within the chapters to recording their journey with the Living Christ.

978-1-57312-677-9 *320 pages/pb* **$19.00**

The Ministry Life
101 Tips for New Ministers
John Killinger

Sharing years of wisdom from more than fifty years in ministry and teaching, *The Ministry Life: 101 Tips for New Ministers* by John Killinger is filled with practical advice and wisdom for a minister's day-to-day tasks as well as advice on intellectual and spiritual habits to keep ministers of any age healthy and fulfilled.

978-1-57312-662-5 *244 pages/pb* **$19.00**

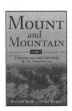

Mount and Mountain
Vol. 1: A Reverend and a Rabbi Talk About the Ten Commandments

Rami Shapiro and Michael Smith

Mount and Mountain represents the first half of an interfaith dialogue—a dialogue that neither preaches nor placates but challenges its participants to work both singly and together in the task of reinterpreting sacred texts. Mike and Rami discuss the nature of divinity, the power of faith, the beauty of myth and story, the necessity of doubt, the achievements, failings, and future of religion, and, above all, the struggle to live ethically and in harmony with the way of God. *978-1-57312-612-0 144 pages/pb* **$15.00**

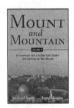

Mount and Mountain
Vol. 2: A Reverend and a Rabbi Talk About the Sermon on the Mount

Rami Shapiro and Michael Smith

This book, focused on the Sermon on the Mount, represents the second half of Mike and Rami's dialogue. In it, Mike and Rami explore the text of Jesus' sermon cooperatively, contributing perspectives drawn from their lives and religious traditions and seeking moments of illumination. *978-1-57312-654-0 254 pages/pb* **$19.00**

Of Mice and Ministers
Musings and Conversations About Life, Death, Grace, and Everything

Bert Montgomery

With stories about pains, joys, and everyday life, *Of Mice and Ministers* finds Jesus in some unlikely places and challenges us to do the same. From tattooed women ministers to saying the "N"-word to the brotherly kiss, Bert Montgomery takes seriously the lesson from Psalm 139—where can one go that God is not already there? *978-1-57312-733-2 154 pages/pb* **$14.00**

Overcoming Adolescence
Growing Beyond Childhood into Maturity

Marion D. Aldridge

In *Overcoming Adolescence*, Marion D. Aldridge poses questions for adults of all ages to consider. His challenge to readers is one he has personally worked to confront: to grow up *all the way*—mentally, physically, academically, socially, emotionally, and spiritually. The key involves not only knowing how to work through the process but also how to recognize what may be contributing to our perpetual adolescence.

978-1-57312-577-2 156 pages/pb **$17.00**

Quiet Faith
An Introvert's Guide to Spiritual Survival
Judson Edwards

In eight finely crafted chapters, Edwards looks at key issues like evangelism, interpreting the Bible, dealing with doubt, and surviving the church from the perspective of a confirmed, but sometimes reluctant, introvert. In the process, he offers some provocative insights that introverts will find helpful and reassuring. *978-1-57312-681-6 144 pages/pb* **$15.00**

Reading Ezekiel (Reading the Old Testament series)
A Literary and Theological Commentary
Marvin A. Sweeney

The book of Ezekiel points to the return of YHWH to the holy temple at the center of a reconstituted Israel and creation at large. As such, the book of Ezekiel portrays the purging of Jerusalem, the Temple, and the people, to reconstitute them as part of a new creation at the conclusion of the book. With Jerusalem, the Temple, and the people so purged, YHWH stands once again in the holy center of the created world.

978-1-57312-658-8 264 pages/pb **$22.00**

Reading Hosea–Micah
(Reading the Old Testament series)
A Literary and Theological Commentary
Terence E. Fretheim

Terence E. Fretheim explores themes of indictment, judgment, and salvation in Hosea–Micah. The indictment against the people of God especially involves issues of idolatry, as well as abuse of the poor and needy. The effects of such behaviors are often horrendous in their severity. While God is often the subject of such judgments, the consequences, like fruit, grow out of the deed itself. *978-1-57312-687-8 224 pages/pb* **$22.00**

Sessions with Genesis (Session Bible Studies series)
The Story Begins
Tony W. Cartledge

Immersing us in the book of Genesis, Tony W. Cartledge examines both its major stories and the smaller cycles of hope and failure, of promise and judgment. Genesis introduces these themes of divine faithfulness and human failure in unmistakable terms, tracing Israel's beginning to the creation of the world and professing a belief that Israel's particular history had universal significance. *978-1-57312-636-6 144 pages/pb* **$14.00**

Sessions with Revelation (Session Bible Studies series)
The Final Days of Evil
David Sapp

David Sapp's careful guide through Revelation demonstrates that it is a letter of hope for believers; it is less about the last days of history than it is about the last days of evil. Without eliminating its mystery, Sapp unlocks Revelation's central truths so that its relevance becomes clear. *978-1-57312-706-6 166 pages/pb* **$14.00**

Silver Linings
My Life Before and After *Challenger 7*
June Scobee Rodgers

We know the public story of *Challenger 7*'s tragic destruction. That day, June's life took a new direction that ultimately led to the creation of the Challenger Center and to new life and new love. Her story of Christian faith and triumph over adversity will inspire readers of every age. *978-1-57312-570-3 352 pages/hc* **$28.00**

978-1-57312-694-6 352 pages/pb **$18.00**

Spacious
Exploring Faith and Place
Holly Sprink

Exploring where we are and why that matters to God is an ongoing process. If we are present and attentive, God creatively and continuously widens our view of the world. *978-1-57312-649-6 156 pages/pb* **$16.00**

The Teaching Church
Congregation as Mentor
Christopher M. Hamlin / Sarah Jackson Shelton

Collected in *The Teaching Church: Congregation as Mentor* are the stories of the pastors who shared how congregations have shaped, nurtured, and, sometimes, broken their resolve to be faithful servants of God. *978-1-57312-682-3 112 pages/pb* **$13.00**

Time for Supper
Invitations to Christ's Table
Brett Younger

Some scholars suggest that every meal in literature is a communion scene. Could every meal in the Bible be a communion text? Could every passage be an invitation to God's grace? At the Lord's Table we experience sorrow, hope, friendship, and forgiveness. These meditations on the Lord's Supper help us listen to the myriad of ways God invites us to gratefully, reverently, and joyfully share the cup of Christ. *978-1-57312-720-2 246 pages/pb* **$18.00**

A Time to Laugh
Humor in the Bible
Mark E. Biddle

An extension of his well-loved seminary course on humor in the Bible, A *Time to Laugh* draws on Mark E. Biddle's command of Hebrew language and cultural subtleties to explore the ways humor was intentionally incorporated into Scripture. With characteristic liveliness, Biddle guides the reader through the stories of six biblical characters who did rather unexpected things. 978-1-57312-683-0 *164 pages/pb* **$14.00**

The World Is Waiting for You
Celebrating the 50th Ordination Anniversary of Addie Davis
Pamela R. Durso & LeAnn Gunter Johns, eds.

Hope for the church and the world is alive and well in the words of these gifted women. Keen insight, delightful observations, profound courage, and a gift for communicating the good news are woven throughout these sermons. The Spirit so evident in Addie's calling clearly continues in her legacy. 978-1-57312-732-5 *224 pages/pb* **$18.00**

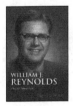

William J. Reynolds
Church Musician
David W. Music

William J. Reynolds is renowned among Baptist musicians, music ministers, song leaders, and hymnody students. In eminently readable style, David W. Music's comprehensive biography describes Reynolds's family and educational background, his career as a minister of music, denominational leader, and seminary professor. 978-1-57312-690-8 *358 pages/pb* **$23.00**

With Us in the Wilderness
Finding God's Story in Our Lives
Laura A. Barclay

What stories compose your spiritual biography? In *With Us in the Wilderness*, Laura Barclay shares her own stories of the intersection of the divine and the everyday, guiding readers toward identifying and embracing God's presence in their own narratives.

978-1-57312-721-9 *120 pages/pb* **$13.00**

To order call **1-800-747-3016** or visit **www.helwys.com**